MONTHERLANT AND SUICIDE

José Porrúa Turanzas, S.A.
EDICIONES

Director General:
JOSÉ PORRÚA VENERO

Sub-director General:
ENRIQUE PORRÚA VENERO

Director:
CONSTANTINO GARCÍA GARVÍA

Executive Director: American Division: BRUNO M. DAMIANI

studia humanitatis

MONTHERLANT AND SUICIDE

CHARLOTTE FRANKEL GERRARD

studia humanitatis

PUBLISHER, PRINTER AND DISTRIBUTOR
José Porrúa Turanzas, S. A.
Cea Bermúdez, 10 - Madrid-3
España

Dep. legal: 33.684

I. S. B. N. 84-7317-063-6

IMPRESO EN ESPAÑA
PRINTED IN SPAIN

Ediciones José Porrúa Turanzas, S. A.
Cea Bermúdez, 10 - Madrid-3

TALLERES GRÁFICOS PORRÚA, S. A.
JOSÉ, 10 - MADRID-29

To my mother
Ida Brazel Frankel (1905-1945)

«Celui qui changerait l'opinion sur le suicide, et améliorerait les façons de se suicider, serait un bienfaiteur de l'humanité — mais tenu pour un monstre. (12 mai 1972)» *

---

* Henry de Montherlant, *Tous feux éteints* (*Carnets 1965, 1966, 1967, Carnets sans dates, Carnets 1972*) (Paris: Gallimard, 1975), p. 171.

CONTENTS

SELECTED BIBLIOGRAPHY

I. Primary Sources

Montherlant, Henry de. *Aux fontaines du désir.* Paris: Bernard Grasset, 1927.

— *Brocéliande* suivi de *L'Art et la vie,* 2e édition. Paris: Gallimard, 1956.

— *Carnets*: *Années 1930 à 1944,* 22e éd. Paris: Gallimard, 1957.

— *Carnets XXII à XXVIII*: *Du 23 Avril 1932 au 22 Novembre 1934* [actually goes to 17 février 1935]. Paris: La Table ronde, 1955.

— *Carnets XLII et XLIII*: *Du 1er Janvier 1942 au 31 Décembre 1943.* Paris: La Table ronde, 1948.

— *Le Chaos et la nuit.* Paris: Gallimard, 1963.

— *Les Garçons.* Paris: Gallimard, 1969.

— *La Guerre civile.* Paris: Gallimard, 1965.

— *Mais aimons-nous ceux que nous aimons?* Paris: Gallimard, 1973.

— *La Marée du soir*: *Carnets 1968-1971.* Paris: Gallimard, 1972.

— *Mors et Vita,* reprinted with *Service inutile.* Paris: Gallimard, 1954.

— *La Petite Infante de Castille.* Paris: Bernard Grasset, 1929.

— *Le Songe* in *Romans.* Paris: Bibliothèque de la Pléiade, 1959.

— «Statement or testament written on May 15, 1972», in *Le Monde* (le 27 septembre 1972), p. 13.

— *Tous feux éteints* (*Carnets 1965, 1966, 1967, Carnets sans dates, Carnets 1972*). Paris: Gallimard, 1975.

— *La Tragédie sans masque.* Paris: Gallimard, 1972.

— *Le Treizième César.* Paris: Gallimard, 1970.

— *Un Assassin est mon maître.* Paris: Gallimard, 1971.

— *Un Voyageur solitaire est un Diable.* Paris: Gallimard, 1961.

— *Va jouer avec cette poussière.* (*Carnets 1958-1964*). Paris: Gallimard, 1966.

II. Secondary Sources

Alvarez, A. *The Savage God, a Study of Suicide.* London: Weidenfeld and Nicholson, 1971, reprinted 1972.

Barrès, Maurice. *Du sang, de la volupté et de la mort.* Paris: Albert Fontemoing, 1903.

Benoist, Alain de. «Thème central: Gabriel Matzneff parle de Montherlant», *Nouvelle Ecole,* no. 20 (septembre-octobre, 1972), pp. 68-77.

Blanc, André. *Montherlant: un pessimisme heureux.* Paris: Editions du Centurion, 1968.

Boisdeffre, Pierre de. «La Fin d'un vrai stoïcien», *Les Nouvelles Littéraires* (du 2 au 8 octobre, 1972), pp. 3-5.

Branan, A. G. Review of *Mais aimons-nous ceux que nous aimons?,* in *French Review,* XLVIII (March 1975), 801.

Cadieu, Martine. «Montherlant, l'ami», *Nouvelle Revue Française* (février 1973), pp. 23-29.

Camus, Albert. *Le Mythe de Sisyphe.* Paris: Collection Idées-Gallimard, 1942 [1966].

D'Ormesson, Jean. «L'équinoxe de septembre», *Nouvelle Revue Française* (février 1973), pp. 40-49.

Durkheim, Emile. *Le Suicide, Etude de sociologie,* nouvelle édition. Paris: Félix Alcan, 1930. Originally published 1897.

Dutourd, Jean. «La Mort de Montherlant», *France-Soir* (24-25 septembre, 1972), p. 6.

Fabre-Luce, Alfred. «Le Suicide de dignité», *Le Monde* (27 septembre, 1972), p. 13.

Farber, Maurice L. *Theory of Suicide.* New York: Funk and Wagnalls, 1968.

Ganne, Gilbert. *Interviews impubliables.* Paris: Plon, 1965.

Hardwick, Elizabeth. *Seduction and Betrayal.* New York: Random House, 1970, reprinted 1974.

Kyria, Pierre. «Montherlant, une fidélité à l'exigence», *Nouvelle Revue Française* (février 1973), pp. 30-33.

Lamartine, Alphonse de. *Raphaël: Pages de la vingtième année.* Paris: Perrotin, 1857.

Lobet, Marcel. «Le suprême exil de Montherlant», *Revue générale,* no. 8 (octobre 1972), pp. 89-93.

Matzneff, Gabriel. «Montherlant éducateur», *Nouvelle Revue Française* (février 1973), pp. 11-16.

Meynard, Léon. *Le Suicide,* 4e édition. Paris: Presses Universitaires de France, 1966.

Montaigne, Michel de. *Œuvres complètes.* Paris: Bibliothèque de la Pléiade, 1962.

Piatier, Jacqueline. «Une Sensibilité bardée de fer», *Le Monde* (23 septembre, 1972), p. 24.

Renauld-Krantz. «Le Chevalier du néant», *Nouvelle Revue Française* (février 1973), pp. 17-22.

Saint Pierre, Michel de. «Montherlant, du rire au désespoir», *Les Nouvelles Littéraires* (du 2 au 8 octobre, 1972), p. 6.

— «Montherlant, mon ami», *Carrefour* (le 27 septembre, 1972), p. 16.

Sienkiewicz, Henryk. *Quo Vadis.* New York: Grosset and Dunlap, originally published 1897, reprinted 1924.

Société Française de Thanatologie. *Mort naturelle et mort violente, Suicide et Sacrifice.* Lyon: Masson et Cie., 1972.

Szasz, Thomas. *The Second Sin.* Garden City, N. Y.: Anchor-Doubleday, 1973.

Touraine, [Yves]. *Le Suicide ascétique.* Paris: Nouvelles Éditions Debresse, 1960.

Vigny, Alfred de. *Journal d'un poète.* Paris: Calmann Lévy, 1882.

Voltaire, (Arouet), François-Marie. *Romans, Contes et Mélanges,* 2 vols. Paris: Livre de Poche, 1972.

PROLOGUE

Albert Camus opens his most famous essay with the striking thought that the only truly important question in philosophy concerns suicide. His examination of the major philosophers of the absurd serves only as an introduction to his refutation of their «leap of faith» (1), but he also declares his general refusal of suicide. While noting certain instances when suicide may be justifiable to save someone or to further a political cause, Camus, for the most part, rejects such a resolution to personal dilemmas. Not so Henry de Montherlant, whose long career includes many literary expressions of the usefulness, nobility, or desirability of self-destruction. Not only as the young *voyageur traqué,* not only as an old man, half-blind, did he discuss suicide, but in his mature period as well:

> On ne réfléchit pas assez au fait que, pendant dix-huit siècles, le christianisme empêchant les Européens de se suicider, il leur a fallu beaucoup plus de courage pour supporter l'adversité qu'il n'en a fallu aux Anciens. Le Moyen Age, la Renaissance, tant

(1) Albert Camus, *Le Mythe de Sisyphe* (Paris: Collection Idées-Gallimard, 1942 [1966]), pp. 53-63.

d'atrocités et pas un suicide! Tout supporté jusqu'au bout, sans fuir! C'est à peser quand on juge les civilisations.

Le jour où, en France, on commence de se suicider —après la Révolution,— on renoue avec le monde qui s'éteignait vers le IIIe siècle (2).

For such an avid admirer of the Romans as Montherlant, that is indeed high praise. He also points out that Lucretius, Seneca, and Petronius killed themselves after contributing new insight into metaphysics, morality, or sensuality (3). Montherlant reports that, in addition to suicide, the Ancient Romans understood homosexuality better than contemporary Frenchmen do.

De nos jours, le suicide est tenu pour fait de neurasthénie, voire de lâcheté, et il crée une sensation d'horreur. Chez les Romains, il est accompli par les hommes les plus posés et les plus dignes: un moment vient où la somme des dégoûts que l'on éprouve ou que l'on attend est par trop supérieure à la somme des agréments; on se tue, et cela est appelé la 'sortie raisonnable' (j'insiste sur le mot 'raisonnable', tout opposé à notre conception moderne, où suicide équivaut plus ou moins à détraquement). On ne nous dit pas que Brutus ou Menenius se suicident dans une crise de dépression nerveuse; on nous dit qu'ils sont vaincus et on nous fait comprendre qu'un ordre s'instaure qu'ils ne veulent pas souffrir; cette raison paraît très suffisante pour justifier qu'ils se donnent la mort.

De nos jours, la pédérastie est tenue pour vice ou, comme le suicide, névrose. Faut-il rappeler qu'Auguste, Jules César, Horace, Virgile... [etc.]...

---

(2) Henry de Montherlant, *Carnets: Années 1930 à 1944*, 22e éd. (Paris: Gallimard, 1957), p. 44.
(3) *Ibid.*, p. 92.

ont été accusés, avec des précisions, d'être *aussi* pédérastes? Ce sont des grands hommes, et ils ont maîtresses, épouses et enfants. Iils sont *aussi* pédérastes, parce qu'ils ne conçoivent pas, et que personne ne conçoit autour d'eux, qu'il soit contraire à la raison de l'être. Toujours la raison. (Variante: Ils sont *aussi* pédérastes et cela n'a aucune importance; ils sont pédérastes sans y penser, ce qui est la seule façon supportable de l'être.)

Rome nous rappelle que suicide et pédérastie sont faits communs chez des hommes parfaitement équilibrés, et l'honneur de leur pays (4).

It is precisely the thesis of the present study that Montherlant's suicide was not an act of mental aberration or of cowardice or pure despair, but rather of lucidity and courage. Before proceeding with Montherlant himself, it is necessary to understand the whole phenomenon of suicide, the attitudes it has traditionally evoked, as well as recent, less emotional reactions.

(4) *Ibid.*, pp. 377-378.

BACKDROP

The general subject of suicide has been discussed by theologians, philosophers, artists, physicians, psychologists, and the average citizen. Often those who have committed suicide are deemed cowardly or sick or weak or deranged. Sometimes they are considered to be transgressors of God's will and criminals in the legal sense. Over the ages, they have been prosecuted, persecuted, and tortured, when they were unsuccessful and thus available for punishment. The Stoics, however, thought them courageous and noble, and even people who regard suicides as pitiable folk make some distinctions, mainly for those who die to save someone else or to uphold a cause. In such cases, however, whether Christians, Communists, or firemen, they are called martyrs, not suicides! Most often, even today, the word is a term of opprobrium. A few researchers, however, offer valuable insights into the phenomenon. Durkheim, in his landmark sociological study, remains, to my mind, the richest. He opens with several definitions and quickly states that suicide is not always a sign of madness (1) and

---

(1) Emile Durkheim, *Le Suicide, Etude de sociologie,* nouvelle édition (Paris: Félix Alcan, 1930), originally published 1897, p. 31;

that in fact, there is an inverse proportion between madness and suicide: women and Jews have a higher rate of mental illness than men and non-Jews, but a lower rate of suicide (pp. 38-40). Likewise he finds no correlation between alcoholism and suicide, since statistically, France has more suicides but fewer alcoholics than Belgium, England, Holland, Sweden, and Russia. Only Denmark has an abundance of both suicide and alcoholism. Within France itself, this holds true (pp. 50-51, p. 47).

Working with heterogeneous populations in Switzerland and the Austro-Hungarian empire, studying Catholics and Protestants, Durkheim concludes that if northern Europeans have a higher incidence than southerners, this predisposition lies not in ethnic causes but in social ones (pp. 62-68). Neither does he accept the notion that climatic factors are the explanation, for in some periods of history, warm climates like Rome and India have had high rates of suicide (p. 83-84). Not heat but light of day seems to be significant, and weekends decrease suicide (pp. 90-101). These facts point to a correlation involving activity, work, and suicide. If daytime is more often than night the setting for suicide, it is because «la vie sociale est le plus intense» (p. 99). Durkheim even discusses the effect of artificial lighting, more common in the city, thus offsetting seasonal effects (p. 104). Not the «physical milieu» but «social conditions» make the difference (p. 106).

In Book II, Durkheim treats social causes and types of suicide. Protestants have more suicides in

---

hereafter, references to this volume will be documented parenthetically in the text.

their midst than Catholics and Jews, not because of a difference in proscription but because, in Catholic society, there is more structure and integration. Likewise, Jews, so often persecuted, have been closely knit and unified (p. 159). He concludes: «Si elle [religion] protège l'homme contre le désir de se détruire, ce n'est pas parce qu'elle lui prêche, avec des arguments *sui generis*, le respect de sa personne; c'est parce qu'elle est une société» (p. 173). More than dogma or ritual, what preserves people best from suicide is the society that is most integrated.

Marriage is another field for Durkheim's research. It becomes clear that the family, *not marriage*, is of value to women. For men, the contrary is true; it is marriage itself that is beneficial (pp. 196-207). In another sphere, that of war, he finds that in times of social commotion, as in «great, popular wars», society becomes more integrated, and there is a decrease in suicide, an individualistic act (pp. 221-223).

Financial crises do seem to be marked by more suicides, but in deflation, suicide is not necessarily low (pp. 264-266). Also noted was a big increase in Italian suicides during such good times as the post-unification period (p. 267). Poor countries or regions like Ireland, Calabria, and Spain are not high in suicides when compared with France (p. 269). Therefore, concludes Durkheim, financial and industrial crises, even when they are marked by suicides, do not prove that poverty causes suicide. Rather «c'est parce qu'elles sont des crises, c'est-à-dire des perturbations de l'ordre collectif» (p. 271). This statement leads into the greatest Durkheim discovery, namely, that in very catastrophic and in very marvellous times, in prosperity as well as in depression, an imbalance occurs that throws people into an abnormal state. Even a time of success, power, and good fortune can do it, can shake up the person to an unbearable degree. Appetites and desires are intense and exalted. «L'état de dérèglement ou d'*anomie* est donc encore renforcé par ce fait que les passions sont moins disciplinées au moment même où elles auraient besoin d'une plus forte discipline» (p. 281). He continues his argument that such a man finds the struggle more violent and painful than usual, as well as less ordered. Suicides increase at such a time (2).

Among Durkheim's great contributions is the evidence of a wealth of types of suicide. In analyzing «suicide égoïste», he discusses the melancholy fellows capable of reflecting, thinking, meditating, and even recording their reactions as they asphyxiate themselves. Then he goes to another type of «suicide égoïste»:

> Le sujet, au lieu de méditer tristement sur son état, en prend allégrement son parti. Il a conscience de son égoïsme et des conséquences qui en découlent logiquement; mais il les accepte par avance et entreprend de vivre comme l'enfant ou l'animal, avec cette seule différence qu'il se rend compte de ce qu'il fait... Sachant qu'il ne peut rien

(2) *Ibid.*, pp. 281-283. «Conjugal anomie» also exists and can lead to divorce or suicide (p. 307). Durkheim arrives at a very interesting observation from his statistics about marriage: that monogamy benefits man not woman, that the wife is the one who has made a sacrifice by marrying (pp. 310-311). Although he probably would be surprised by the types of jobs some women are doing today, he already felt that the answer to «conjugal anomie» was a change in the life of women, that they should become more involved in society, as men already were. He was right in stressing that, while women would retain certain differences, psychological inequality of the sexes had to be fought and corrected. «Pour que l'homme et la femme puissent être également protégés par la même institution, il faut, avant tout, qu'ils soient des êtres de même nature» (p. 444).

espérer d'autre, il ne demande rien de plus, tout disposé, s'il est empêché d'atteindre cette unique fin, à se défaire d'une existence désormais sans raison. C'est le suicide épicurien. Car Epicure n'ordonnait pas à ses disciples de hâter la mort, il leur conseillait, au contraire, de vivre tant qu'ils y trouvaient quelque intérêt... il les exhortait à se tenir toujours prêts à en sortir, au moindre appel des circonstances. Ici donc, la mélancolie philosophique et rêveuse est remplacée par un sang-froid sceptique et désabusé qui est particulièrement sensible à l'heure du dénouement. Le patient se frappe sans haine, sans colère, mais aussi sans cette satisfaction morbide avec laquelle l'intellectuel savoure son suicide. Il est, encore plus que ce dernier, sans passion. Il n'est pas surpris de l'issue à laquelle il aboutit; c'est un événement qu'il prévoyait comme plus ou moins prochain. Aussi ne s'ingénie-t-il pas en de longs préparatifs; d'accord avec sa vie antérieure, il cherche seulement à diminuer la douleur. Tel est notamment le cas de ces viveurs qui, quand le moment inévitable est arrivé où ils ne peuvent plus continuer leur existence facile, se tuent avec une tranquillité ironique et une sorte de simplicité (pp. 318-319).

It seems to this writer that Henry de Montherlant, both in his life and in his work, treats the notion of suicide in this way.

At the time of Montherlant's suicide, a number of articles appeared in which the following expressions recurred: «Roman» (3), «triumph» (4), and «Stoïc»

(3) Jean Dutourd, «La Mort de Montherlant», *France-Soir* (24-25 septembre, 1972), p. 6: «Il n'était ni fou, ni névrosé, ni, Dieu sait! gâteux... Le revolver de Montherlant, c'est le glaive de Caton ou de Brutus.»

(4) See Alfred Fabre-Luce, «Le Suicide de dignité», *Le Monde* (27 septembre, 1972), p. 13. Therein, Montherlant's suicide is designated «la signature du dernier acte, le triomphe sur la mort par le choix de l'heure».

(5). On the day he died, he wrote three letters, one of which was partially quoted in an article by the recipient: «Je tiens beaucoup à vos deux mots: 'lucidité' et 'dignité'» (6). It would seem that Montherlant's suicide does not resemble that of Ernest Hemingway, whose attachment to Spain and to bullfighting paralleled Montherlant's. While Hemingway supposedly broke «down into psychosis» with attendant «persecutory delusions», Montherlant was not mentally ill at all. The term «psychotic suicide» (7) is then inappropriate to Montherlant's act. What would be applicable is the following statement:

> The final act of suicide is basically a resolution, a movement, perceived as the only possible one, out of a life situation felt to be unbearable by one of low sense of competence, with hope extinguished.
>
> It is finally action, no longer just feeling. Often there seems to be an element of assertion here, an active rebellion against the passive acceptance of difficulties, a declaration of independence. It is as if the victim cries: «*At least I am competent to do this!*» (8).

---

(5) Jacqueline Piatier, «Une Sensibilité bardée de fer», *Le Monde* (23 septembre, 1972), p. 24: «... sa mort d'aujourd'hui fait du stoïcisme une profession de foi.» Also, Pierre de Boisdeffre, «La Fin d'un vrai stoïcien», *Les Nouvelles Littéraires* (du 2 au 8 octobre, 1972: «Hommage à Montherlant»), pp. 3-5. On the last page, Boisdeffre says that Montherlant rejected the notion that a man who commits suicide is «un 'vaincu'... Il fallait innocenter le suicide, lui restituer sa dignité».

(6) Quoted by Michel de Saint Pierre, «Montherlant, du rire au désespoir», in *Les Nouvelles Littéraires, op. cit.*, p. 6.

(7) Maurice L. Farber, *Theory of Suicide* (New York: Funk and Wagnalls, 1968), pp. 31-32.

(8) *Ibid.*, p. 42.

With «the decline of one's powers and the inevitable imminence of death» comes a reduction of hope (9). The last word is no more a compliment in Montherlant's lexicon than in Camus' or Anouilh's, but the statement is consonant with Montherlant's frequent emphasis on suicide as a valid procedure when his physical and creative powers would have run their course. According to Gabriel Matzneff, all Montherlant's friends knew that he would kill himself to avoid complete dependence on nurses or friends, were he to be faced with paralysis and total blindness (10). Another friend, Michel de Saint Pierre, repeats Montherlant's refusal to become a burden to anyone. Saint Pierre also reproduces, from the suicide note he received, Montherlant's statement that his periods of blindness occasionally lasted several hours and «quelquefois des jours entiers» (11).

Actually, the crux of the matter is here, for Montherlant always rated sensual pleasure, literary creativity, and continued existence in that order. In other words, if one can no longer enjoy physical experiences and if one's ability to write will be hampered, life will cease to be desirable. This is not to say that when Montherlant took his own life, he was in the depths of despair. Rather, a thorough study of Montherlant's opinions on death, and on suicide in particular, suggests he killed himself with

---

(9) *Ibid.*, p. 92.

(10) «Thème central: Gabriel Matzneff parle de Montherlant, entretien recueilli par Alain de Benoist», *Nouvelle Ecole*, n.º 20 (septembre-octobre, 1972), p. 76.

(11) *Loc. cit.* Also, see «Montherlant, mon ami», *Carrefour* (le 27 septembre, 1972), p. 16. Montherlant had explicitly stated that he knew how to depart from life «avec élégance».

a mixture of dispassionate lucidity and passionate appreciation of what is precious in life--love, desire, and intensity of experience. This process of reconciliation of opposites is faithful to Montherlant's lifelong principle «Syncrétisme et alternance» (12). Paradoxes and seeming contradictions are the stuff of which Montherlant was made. Despite the works in which figure priests, nuns, and archbishops, Montherlant's thought belongs to the tradition of the skeptics, the Stoïcs, and the men of reason. Consequently, before focussing on Montherlant's many expressions of opinion on suicide, it is advisable to flash back to the maker of modern French thought, to that human bridge between the ancient world and the modern, to the founder of a literary genre--to Michel de Montaigne.

In the third essay of Book II, the great Renaissance author treats suicide as «Coustume de l'Isle de Cea» and calls it nature's greatest gift, «la clef des champs», and the most beautiful kind of death. «La vie despend de la volonté d'autruy; la mort, de la nostre» (13). Montaigne declares that God permits it in such circumstances when «le vivre nous est pire que le mourir» (14). The last sentence reads: «La douleur insupportable et une pire mort me semblent les plus excusables incitations» (15). Yet the sentence most ap-

---

(12) First elucidated in 1925; see *Aux fontaines du désir* (Paris: Bernard Grasset, 1927), pp. 23-46.

(13) Michel de Montaigne, *Œuvres complètes* (Paris: Bibliothèque de la Pléiade, 1962), p. 331.

(14) *Ibíd.*, p. 332.

(15) *Ibíd.*, p. 343. According to Gabriel Matzneff, *op. cit.*, p. 70, Montherlant was extremely irritated by philosophers who argue that physical pain is an illusion that can be overcome by reason.

propriate to Montherlant occurs one page before: it is Montaigne's observation that suicide should not be classified automatically as an act of despair. Indeed, it may be brought about by «la chaleur de l'espoir..., et souvent une tranquille et rassise inclination de jugement». It is the last description that seems to fit Montherlant's case. While he tried to dissuade the very young from suicide, encouraging them to study life a bit first to test whether they wished to part from it (16), he condoned suicide and even admired it in mature people, provided it was accomplished consciously, lucidly, thoughtfully, premeditatedly, and coolly.

One of the descendants of the Stoic tradition in French literature, Alfred de Vigny, had the youthful intention of studying the problem of suicide, its types and causes. This unrealized project was to have expressed his «ideas on life». Vigny felt that the absence of hope was salutary and that indeed «*L'espérance est la plus grande de nos folies*» (17). If one expects nothing, «le moindre bouquet, la plus petite feuille, réjouit la vue et le coeur, on en sait gré à la puissance qui a permis qu'elle se rencontrât sous vos pas» (p. 30). Wisdom, said Vigny, was synonymous with «Un désespoir paisible, sans convulsions de colère et sans reproches au ciel» (p. 32). Vigny, in his early thirties, noted in this journal the examples of Romans

---

(16) Henry de Montherlant, *Le Treizième César* (Paris: Gallimard, 1970), pp. 47-48. In addition, see Gabriel Matzneff, «Montherlant éducateur», *Nouvelle Revue Française* (février 1973), p. 15, in which he credits Montherlant with preventing him from yielding to the fascination of «l'abîme du suicide».

(17) *Journal d'un poète* (Paris: Calmann Lévy, 1882), p. 29. Further quotations from this volume will appear parenthetically in the text.

like Cato who killed himself and even contemporaneous events such as the following account of an admirable suicide:

> Un lieutenant au 6e de la garde, ayant reçu l'ordre de faire feu, a refusé parce que la rue était pleine de femmes et d'enfants. Le colonel réitère l'ordre de faire feu et le menace de le faire arrêter, il prend un pistolet et se brûle la cervelle (p. 50).

Although Vigny seems to have had more of the milk of human kindness than Montherlant, there is a striking similarity between their expressions of distaste for mediocrity and their yearning for flight (Vigny, pp. 53-54). In artistic matters too, Vigny had his doubts about best--sellers, hit plays, and immediately admired painters (p. 92). A notation made by Vigny in 1834 could easily pass for a *pensée* by Montherlant a century later: «Les masses vont en avant comme les troupeaux d'aveugles en Egypte, frappant indifféremment de leurs bâtons imbéciles ceux qui les repoussent, ceux qui les détournent et ceux qui les devancent sur le grand chemin» (p. 94). Julien l'Apostat, convinced that he was way ahead of the «masses stupides et grossières» decides to let himself be killed in Persia (an 1836 notation, p. 106). As for «modern» man, Vigny saw him as wishing God existed but doubting that He did (p. 264). Skepticism and Stoicism flow on in Vigny's veins as they did in Seneca's and in Montaigne's. In Vigny's case, there is also the dramatic theme of suicide, that of the man who is superior morally and esthetically. The notable illustration is of course Chatterton the poet, but Vigny's hero is not entirely historically accurate.

Another Romantic treatment of the theme of self-destruction is of less importance than *Chatterton*: Lamartine's *Raphaël,* which presents a rejection of suicide (18). The heroine, Julie, has certain obvious resemblances to the heroine of *La Nouvelle Héloïse*: for example, her name, and the fact she is married, although Wolmar is a more conjugal figure than the old husband in Lamartine's novel. Also, his hero and heroine refer, in chapters LIX, LX, and LXI, to Rousseau and Mme de Warens. Furthermore, in chapter LXXX, Raphaël identifies himself with Jean-Jacques. What is significant for the present study, however, is the heroine's atheism, which changes under the young man's influence.

Before this transformation, Julie is embarrassed by Raphaël's evocation of God. She explains that she has learned from her teachers that God is a marvellous but empty illusion, and yet, in seemingly Deistic fashion she seems to believe in a God that created Nature. The Infinite in which she believes is Law not God. Prayer seems pointless to her since she does not accept the idea of revelation or rapport between humanity and some manifestation of the Infinite Being. It is quite a romantic scene that frames her exclamation to Raphaël, as they go sailing along: «'Oh! mourons!... la terre n'a rien de plus à nous dònner, le ciel rien de plus à nous promettre!'» (p. 155). She wants them to kill themselves for the same reason that, so many years later, Gide's Olivier in *Les Faux-Monnayeurs* will speak of suicide performed at the

(18) A[lphonse] de Lamartine, *Raphaël: Pages de la vingtième année* (Paris: Perrotin, 1857), especially pp. 131-138, 154-159, 265-266, 306-309, 350-351. Direct quotations will be documented parenthetically in the text, although all the references are from the afore-mentioned pages.

moment of supreme happiness. Lyrically describing the beauty that surrounds them, Julie suggests that the mountains reflected in the lake cast shadows to beckon them to extinction with these words:

> «Ensevelissez-vous dans ce linceul que je vous tends»; ... Aucun oeil humain ne nous voit. Nul ne saura par quel mystère la barque vide ira demain échouer sur quelque rocher de la côte... Oh! mourons dans cette ivresse de l'âme et de la nature, qui ne nous fera sentir de la mort que sa volupté! Plus tard, nous voudrons mourir et nous mourrons peut-être moins heureux! (pp. 155-156).

So persuasive is Julie that even the devout Raphaël almost yields to the temptation of suicide, but her fainting fit breaks the spell. Subsequently, she finds that love proves God's existence because the joy she feels is greater than any earthly happiness. Even jealousy will never rear its ugly head, she writes in a last letter, urging Raphaël to find another woman to love after her own death. While the novel lacks verisimilitude in the portions dealing with Raphaël's adoration of Julie's aged husband, its theme of suicide and the depiction of noble skeptics are pertinent to our study. Despite Lamartine's Christian ending, the unchristian elements stand out with honor and dignity, for the old husband is described as intelligent, altruistic, and admirable. Montherlant's own works in which Catholicism figures have often given rise to naïve suppositions of his basic faith; in his case, what is at work is rather his fascination with different types of character and situation, as well as his principle of «Syncrétisme et alternance». In all events, the Romantic works discussed here have been included because of Montherlant's interest in that literary period and because of their emphasis on suicide and Stoicism.

A contemporary statement about suicide is the complimentary one by literary critic Elizabeth Hardwick, who calls the self-inflicted deaths of writers Sylvia Plath and Yukio Mishima actions that assert themselves «as a value, a definition, a pure leap» (19). Specifically of Sylvia Plath, she writes: «Suicide is an assertion of power, of the strength —not the weakness— of the personality. She is no poor animal sneaking away, giving up; instead she is strong, threatening, dangerous» (20). As for Virginia Woolf and her «madness», the critic writes: «Her suicide was of the heroic kind; she expressed the determination not to drag others through it once more» (21).

Another literary critic, A. Alvarez, devotes the major part of his fascinating treatment of suicide and literature to Sylvia Plath. Most of his opinions run counter to those of Elizabeth Hardwick or Montherlant, but they merit attention because of the references to rationality and Stoïcism. According to Alvarez,

> First and most important, suicide is a closed world with its own irresistible logic. This is not to say that people commit suicide, as the Stoics did, coolly, deliberately, as a rational choice between rational alternatives. The Romans may have disciplined themselves into accepting this frigid logic

---

(19) *Seduction and Betrayal* (New York: Random House, 1970, reprinted 1974), p. 113.
(20) *Ibid.*, p. 112.
(21) *Ibid.*, p. 137.

> but those who have done so in modern history are, in the last analysis, monsters.
>
> The logic of suicide is, then, not rational in the old Stoic sense. It scarcely could be since there is almost no one now, even among the philosophers, who believes that reason is clean and straightforward, or that motives can ever be less than equivocal (22).

However, whether Alvarez thinks it impossible or not, Montherlant's lifelong admiration of the Romans and his rigid principles about quality, independence, and individuality seem to explain his act and preclude the explanation of monstrosity. What would win Montherlant's approval is the observation that suicide is neither a disease nor a sin. For Alvarez, it transcends morality as well as «social or psychic prophylaxis» (23).

Some other contemporary studies of suicide are less well written but more statistical. A meeting in Lyon on June 2 and 3, 1972 produced statistics and papers dealing with suicide. Annual figures for France range from 8000 in one report to 14,000 in another (24). Suicide by burning in Vietnam and Czechoslovakia was striking for political reasons but also inspired similar acts elsewhere for personal motives (25). A big section on Africa takes issue with Durkheim's emphasis on societal integration as a deterrent to suicide, since in Africa city-dwellers

(22) *The Savage God, a Study of Suicide* (London: Weidenfeld and Nicolson, 1971, reprinted 1972), p. 105.

(23) *Ibid.*, p. 237.

(24) Société Française de Thanatologie, *Mort naturelle et mort violente, Suicide et Sacrifice* (Lyon: Masson et Cie., 1972), p. 114.

(25) *Ibid.*, p. 152.

commit suicide less frequently than in villages where presumably the community pressures and structures are closer (26). Professor Thomas of Paris is convinced, therefore, that «on ne peut plus se fier à Durkheim» (27).

Another recent book is interesting for its references to suicide and French literature (28). Meynard refers to Montaigne, Montesquieu, Rousseau, and Voltaire, but when he reaches existentialism with Sartre and Heidegger, it becomes obvious that he considers suicide an unauthentic act of *mauvaise foi* (pp. 25-26). He entitles one chapter, «Suicide et courage», finding these terms mutually exclusive (p.38). Likewise in a chapter called «Suicide et sacrifice», he makes too much of a distinction between «l'acte de se donner la mort et l'acte d'offrir sa vie» (p. 61). The ending is clearly religious (p. 119). Meynard belongs to those moralizers who consider suicide an error or crime (29).

Very different in outlook, Touraine compares the freedom implicit in suicide, a refusal of fate, to the magic of Christian ritual. He likens suicide to baptism, confession, and extreme unction, for they all partake of magic (pp. 45-46). He asks whether we cannot find a more honorable and dignified way to «disappear» than by going down-hill to decrepitude, inviting sadness, pity, shame, scorn, hatred, or euthanasia. Suicide is a discreet and efficient method (pp.

---

(26) *Ibíd.*, p. 171.

(27) *Ibíd.*, p. 177.

(28) Léon Meynard, *Le Suicide*, 4e édition (Paris: Presses Universitaires de France, 1966). References to this volume will appear parenthetically in the text.

(29) [Yves] Touraine, *Le Suicide ascétique* (Paris: Nouvelles Éditions Debresse, 1960), p. 26. References to this volume will appear parenthetically in the text.

60-61). Such an interpretation is most appropriate for Montherlant. Touraine, in developing his theory of ascetic suicide, hails Socrates as a precursor (p. 70). He also respects an anonymous work of the eighteenth century which claimed that suicide was a manifestation of Divine providence (pp. 71-75). Moving into the next century, he describes the last night of the year 1829, when Alphonse Rabbe purposely took an overdose of the opium he legitimately possessed for treating an incurable disease. In his last letters, Rabbe claimed to be calm and dignified, not a coward (pp. 76-77).

An even more deliberate example Touraine gives of ascetic suicide is the death of Socialist Paul Lafargue, at about sixty-nine years of age, on November 28, 1911 (pp. 77-78). In discussing this case, Touraine makes an eloquent apology for suicide, lucidly committed:

> A cet âge où les buts que l'on s'est donnés disparaissent un à un, où les raisons de vivre et la sensibilité s'amenuisent jusqu'à devenir inexistantes, il n'est pas de solution qui soit plus conforme à un certain idéal de la mort chez des individus appartenant à une civilisation qui, dans d'autres domaines, a su maîtriser la fatalité de la nature (pp. 80-81).

While Touraine calls atheists the most forsaken of men, he praises in them «un certain orgueil prométhéen», for they most passionately assert themselves (p. 101). Those atheists who kill themselves merit respect, says Touraine, for they do not seek pity. Instead they are facing nothingness quite consciously (p. 112). Death is in itself rather ordinary; it happens to all animals, but the suppression of self is exclusively human (p. 114). Ascetic suicide can be defined as «une tentative de contrôle et de maîtrise de soi afin d'épargner à son être l'enlisement dans le non-être et la dégradation de l'idée de soi chez les autres hommes» (p. 114). He concludes that unlike other forms of suicide, the ascetic variety is «une des plus hautes expressions de l'affirmation en la valeur de la vie» (p. 115).

In concluding this examination of the general subject of suicide as an introduction to Montherlant's particular views, it would be possible to add his death to the examples in Touraine's essay. Yet Durkheim's table listing and describing three forms of suicide still provides useful categories and structures for understanding Montherlant's ultimate act. His probable type can be discerned in the characterization of the second kind of «suicide égoïste»: «Sang-froid désabusé du sceptique». Otherwise he might be seen as being of mixed type: «suicide ego-altruiste» and described as «Mélancolie tempérée par une certaine fermeté morale» (30). Although Montherlant's history and literature are evidence of constant interest in the topic, the deed itself occurred when he was of advanced years. As Durkheim showed throughout his sociological landmark, suicide is not a disease; neither should it be a crime. With understanding, he wrote: «Toutes choses égales, c'est à mesure qu'il [l'homme] avance en âge qu'il y devient plus accessible [au suicide], sans doute parce qu'il faut des expériences répétées pour l'amener à sentir tout le vide d'une existence égoïste ou toute la vanité des ambitions sans terme» (31).

(30) Emile Durkheim, *Le Suicide*, p. 332.
(31) *Ibid.*, p. 368.

SENSUALITY AND CREATIVITY

Not only did Montherlant kill himself, but he wrote of suicide many times over many years. He even summarized that aspect of his work in these terms:

> Le suicide permet d'échapper à la vie; il ne permet pas d'échapper à la caricature posthume, et notamment à la caricature, par légèreté ou passion, des raisons de votre suicide...
>
> J'ai honoré le suicide dès l'âge de trente ans, dans *Aux fontaines du désir* ('La mort de Peregrinos'). Puis dans *Service inutile* ('Un sens perdu'). Dans mes *Carnets 1930-1944*. Dans *Brocéliande*, où le héros se tue. Dans *Le Préfet Spendius* [inédit], où les deux héros se tuent. Dans *La Guerre civile*, où, conformément à l'histoire, tous (ou presque) les personnages *bien* se tuent, après la chute du rideau. Dans *Va jouer avec cette poussière*. Dans cet ouvrage-ci. Sept ouvrages (1).

---

(1) *Le Treizième César* (Paris: Gallimard, 1970), pp. 34-35. Of this list, the two plays seem of less importance thematically than the essays, which offer direct authorial opinions, and indeed they are of less interest theatrically than other plays which Montherlant wrote on other subjects. On the other hand, Montherlant's late fiction not only is stylistically excellent, but it is thematically rich in its treatment of death in general, as well as in revealing the author's *état d'âme*. From an earlier time, an essay, *Un Voyageur solitaire est un diable*, helps to understand how this versatile writer views the greatest human predicament.

A skeptic at the very least, Montherlant lightens the mood considerably by his irony, suggesting that he could write a suicide handbook in five easy lessons (2).

More seriously, in «Lecture de Sénèque», Henry de Montherlant reiterates Seneca's remark about the suicide of senile people or those who know they have an incurable malady. Montherlant's comment is poignant as he wonders how one judges the incurable and whether one ought to «'devancer un peu l'inévitable, dans la crainte de ne plus pouvoir le faire au moment où cela sera nécessaire'» (3). From Petronius in *Quo Vadis,* Montherlant quotes: «'Celui qui a su vivre doit savoir mourir'» (4). Furthermore, Montherlant mentions that Petronius' last toast is to Aphrodite, adding this comment:

> Ainsi la «leçon» de *Quo Vadis* peut-elle être que l'amour est le seul objet qui vaille d'être considéré avec un esprit religieux. Cette vue parfaitement intelligente, reçue dès ma neuvième année, ne m'a jamais quitté depuis, et ne me quittera qu'à l'heure où mon esprit me quittera pour toujours, —à moins qu'il ne faille remplacer «mon esprit» par «mes sens» (5).

Inspired to read the English translation of the Polish classic, the present writer was especially struck by the light-hearted suicide of Petronius, a more complex character than the young hero. «Petronius burst into

---

(2) *Le Treizième César,* pp. 43-44.

(3) *Ibíd.,* pp. 93-94.

(4) *Ibíd.,* p. 174. This same quotation already figured in Montherlant's *Va jouer avec cette poussière, Carnets 1958-1964* (Paris: Gallimard, 1966), p. 199, with this personal comment: «Capital. L'art de vivre et l'art de mourir solidaires».

(5) *Le Treizième César,* p. 177.

a laugh so genuine and so gay, that it seemed as if the whole matter were merely an innocent joke.» Then he held out his arm to be lanced by the Greek doctor (6).

This tone of *joie-de-vivre* in the face of death, as well as the tribute to the Goddess of Love, were integral parts of Montherlant's appreciation of *Quo Vadis.* The elevation of the senses above the intellect was a constant in Montherlant's life and writing. Indeed, for Montherlant, the creative artist requires pleasure and independence; they are features first of life, then of work. Beyond them, there is nothing. So states Montherlant in a speech in 1937. Man has a certain span of hours to live. «Il s'agit d'abord, pour tout être, de bien discerner ce qui lui importe par-dessus tout, et là-dessus l'artiste qui nous occupe n'a pas d'hésitation: il y a la vie, puis l'oeuvre, puis rien» (7). This ranking of values is unchanged by time. In his *Carnets,* he honors «le goût du plaisir sexuel et le goût de la création littéraire» and adds the following notation:

> Le jour où, l'âge venu, ces deux forces me manqueront, que me restera-t-il?
> Rien. Il me restera de mourir (8).

This quotation from the end of the volume seems representative of other thoughts throughout the note-

---

(6) Henryk Sienkiewicz, *Quo Vadis* (New York: Grosset and Dunlap, originally published 1897, reprinted 1924), p. 592.

(7) See *Brocéliande,* suivi de *L'Art et la vie,* 2e édition (Paris: Gallimard, 1956), p. 160.

(8) *Années 1930 à 1944,* 22e édition (Paris: Gallimard, 1957), pp. 382-383. Further references to this volume will appear parenthetically in the text.

books. In the very first sentences (p. 13), Montherlant credits «une demi-heure de plaisir physique, donnée par mon semblable», with banishing thoughts of suicide. But if physical love and work were to become impossible, there would always be suicide, an honorable course.

In another observation on sex and creativity, Montherlant in his maturity ponders what might deteriorate first:

> ... ou sa vitalité, ou sa faculté créatrice. Si c'est sa faculté créatrice, il lui reste à consacrer ses dernières années à jouir de la vie, autant que faire se peut. Si c'est sa vitalité, et s'il n'est plus soutenu que par la création, le jour où celle-ci se tarira, il sera vraiment mort, mort de tous côtés; il sera un mort vivant (pp. 365-366).

He added that he differs from other people who live for vanity and money; he claims he lives «uniquement pour la sensualité et pour faire des créations littéraires» (p. 366). His pride in himself is obvious, his scorn for the mass of humankind equally obvious. He respects himself and respects those who respect themselves. Such people may prefer death for that very reason. He describes a case in point from a classical Japanese Noh drama whose theme is a love suicide. Chikamatsu's hero tells the heroine he realizes she is killing herself for him. She replies: «'Non. Je ne le fais que par respect pour moi-même!'» (p. 90).

In a recently published work, there is further evidence of Montherlant's respect for people who commit suicide. Speaking personally, he refutes the notion that these last years were miserable or that he was conscious of being an exile from others, a stranger:

> Il y a pour chaque être un grand nombre de choses auxquelles il ne participe pas. De même pour moi. Mais, toutes les choses auxquelles je n'ai pas de part, je n'y ai pas de part parce que je l'ai voulu ainsi expressément. De sorte que les conclusions pathétiques et romantiques que l'on voudrait tirer de cette notion d'exil, en ce qui me regarde, ne seraient que de la littérature, sans rapport avec la réalité (9).

His dramatic character, Persilès, in *Brocéliande,* is discussed in several passages written in 1955 and 1956. His suicide is seen as courageous, proud, genuine, and heroic (10). In addition, Montherlant speaks of the nobility of the self-destructive heroes of *La Guerre civile* (11). Montherlant's tone reflects his personal stance: cool, reasoned, and unsentimental. This is not the tone of existential anguish.

Certainly the tone in *Va jouer avec cette poussière* is calm, completely lucid, not morbid. He makes an analogy between society's reaction to suicide and its attitude towards sexual deviation. In completely unreasonable fashion, «l'humanité» has usually treated suicide and sexual deviation as crimes. Seneca's enlightened attitude towards suicide did not effect a lasting reform; during the seventeenth and eighteenth centuries, «le cadavre du suicidé, attaché par les pieds à une charrette, était traîné par les rues, la face tournée contre terre, puis le corps pendu par les pieds, et jeté enfin à la voirie...» (12). In fact, on that very page, Montherlant writes an eloquent apology of

(9) *La Tragédie sans masque* (Paris: Gallimard, 1972), p. 148.
(10) *Ibid.*, pp. 174-179 *passim.*
(11) *Ibid.*, pp. 267, 269 and 285.
(12) *Va jouer avec cette poussière* (Paris: Gallimard, 1966), p. 118. Indeed, the pages 118-120 are devoted to the topic of suicide.

suicide; it is an act that honors reason and life when it occurs in old age or illness, «quand votre vie a cessé de pouvoir être digne de vous». He declares that man has the right to end a life he never sought. He also takes exception to the view of suicide as «un acte de vaincu» (13). For Montherlant, a better definition would be that suicide is a challenge, an individual's assertion that he has controlled his own life (14). Obviously, Montherlant's view is non-religious, and indeed the only divinities he would allow to approach a deathbed are: Courage, Desire, and Reason, the latter akin to Indifference and acknowledging that after death there is absolutely nothing (15).

In these later years, Montherlant's maxims and *pensées* (16) continue to deal with the subject of suicide, but the general theme of death is not neglected. For example, he claims to have rid himself of the horror of death by composing *Le Chaos et la nuit*. In fact, in some of these entries, Montherlant seems quite Stoic and heralds the coming of death as a natural ending to «earthly adventure». He comments: «Tout

---

(13) *Ibid.*, p. 119. In fact, I myself regard the general opinion as at best a platitude, more likely a fallacy.

(14) In a controversial book criticizing the tyranny of much psychiatry, Thomas Szasz, himself a psychiatrist, devotes two pages to suicide, which he defines as «a fundamental human right. This does not mean it is morally desirable. It only means that society does not have the moral right to interfere, by force, with a person's decision to commit this act... causing one's own death should be called 'suicide' only by those who disapprove of it; and should be called 'death control' by those who approve of it--or at least do not condemn it». See *The Second Sin* (Garden City, N. Y.: Anchor-Doubleday, 1973), pp. 67-68.

(15) *Va jouer avec cette poussière,* p. 124. This particular thought was written on August 20, 1963, nine years, one month, and one day before his own suicide.

(16) *La Marée du soir*: *Carnets 1968-1971* (Paris: Gallimard, 1972). The page references for this volume will appear parenthetically in the text.

est très bien ainsi. J'ai été un homme de plaisir d'abord, ensuite un créateur littéraire, et ensuite rien. Le plaisir est pris; les oeuvres, c'est pour me faire plaisir aussi que je les faisais, et ce plaisir lui aussi est pris. C'est pourquoi tout est bien ainsi» (p. 16). This is not to say that, in this passage, Montherlant is seeking death; no, but, at the time of the accident that took from him the vision of one eye, he is supremely aware that for him, *life* must mean carnal desire and artistic expression. He refuses to spare the other eye «Car plutôt ne pas être, que ne pas être ce qu'on est fait pour être» (p. 17). He has begun to fall down, once in the Comédie Française, once in a sordid street (pp. 25-26). He is tempted to destroy his unpublished writings (p. 76) and draws an analogy with suicide. Both acts are partially free. One is doomed to die but by committing suicide, the time is freely chosen. Inevitably, one's work is forgotten, but by destroying it, the writer chooses the part and the time: «C'est, comme avec le suicide, une parcelle de liberté dans la nécessité» (p. 77). While the note is not precisely dated, it was written in 1969 upon re-reading one dated August 13, 1969.

However, it is perhaps wise to pay respect to chronology and to appreciate how long Montherlant was interested in the subject of suicide. Let us then follow his advice and notice what he wrote on the last page of «La Mort de Peregrinos» (17), an essay which was composed between 1921 and 1926:

---

(17) In *Aux fontaines du désir* (Paris: Bernard Grasset, 1927), pp. 47-84.

> ... il entra, par la porte du feu, dans les majestés de la disparition totale. Par là il se rapproche davantage encore de nous qui, ne pouvant avoir de foi, ni cependant nous passer de grandeur, rêvons à ce que cela pourrait être de mourir volontairement pour une cause à laquelle nous ne croirions pas. La vraie grandeur, celle qui est complètement vaine, qui ne nous sera comptée nulle part.

What is of special interest in connection with the question of the morality of suicide is precisely the gratuitousness of the act. Peregrinos killed himself for the gesture, to leave his mark, to be different. It is perhaps proper, before leaving this earliest literary expression on suicide, to notice the kind that is involved. Peregrinos the sensual, the parricide, the Christian convert and apostate, would not be an «altruistic suicide», in the Durkheimian ledger. The act was rather one of extreme individualism, growing out of pride and desire for glory. Hence, he fits the description Durkheim gave of the «suicide égoïste» (18).

---

(18) Emile Durkheim, *Le Suicide, Etude de sociologie,* nouvelle édition (Paris: Félix Alcan, 1930, originally published 1897), pp. 223-224, 288-289. Durkheim's definition of «le suicide égoïste» seems very appropriate to Montherlant's case: «L'individualisme excessif n'a pas seulement pour résultat de favoriser l'action des causes suicidogènes, il est, par lui-même, une cause de genre» (p. 224). Durkheim (pp. 288-289) defines and contrasts it with the altruistic and anomic forms, finding some parallels between the anomic and egoistic. In both, the individual does not care very much about society. The egoistical one lacks collective action, while the anomic suicide lacks a societal rein on the passions. «Suicide égoïste» is more common to intellectuals, «suicide anomique» to business leaders. Other Durkheimian insights that seem important in understanding Montherlant's view of suicide are the comparison and contrast between «suicide anomique» and «suicide égoïste». However, they can occur together, and upon occasion, even altruism can combine with *anomie.* In some cases, altruism can unite with egoism, its seeming opposite (pp. 325-326). The last combination applies in «suicide stoïcien», for the Stoic raises individualism to

There is only one other passage from *Aux fontaines du désir* that I find pertinent to our discussion: «J'ai d'ailleurs cessé de m'intéresser beaucoup à moi-même. Je m'intéressais quand j'étais une bête de chasse. A présent que je ne suis plus cela, faute d'appétit, je n'ai plus cette idée exaltante de ma personne qui me faisait considérer la mort avec horreur». It seems that here we have the perfect suicide note, but there is one problem: the words are from «L'ennui à Aranjuez», written in 1925! (19). Furthermore, the young Montherlant envisaged a moment that men face in middle-age or later when «tous pouvaient dire: 'Je ne trouverai rien de plus exquis que ce que j'ai trouvé'. Et là-dessus beaucoup se tuaient, décidément sans ardeur pour une vie baissée de ton... Hélas! ces romantiques, mal lus, pas lus du tout, je me reconnais leur fils ingrat». The romantic, the Stoic are two predecessors admired by Montherlant. He loved the Romans but also read and quoted Chateaubriand and Vigny (20). Yet this admiration did not prevent him from criticizing in both Hugo and Chateaubriand what he considered pretenses and pretensions, democratic as well as aristocratic. He specifically mentions their «cabotinage» (21). This is a good example of Montherlant's reconciliation of opposites, of his life-principle, of «Syncrétisme et alternance».

Leaving *Aux fontaines du désir* but continuing to study the young Montherlant, we find a nearly con-

---

the highest degree, yet makes the human being a dependent part of universal reason, which he serves as a mere instrument (p. 327). Montherlant could also fit into this framework.

(19) In *Aux fontaines du désir*, p. 173.

(20) *Ibid.*, pp. 175-176.

(21) See *Service inutile* in *Mors et Vita*, reprinted with *Service inutile* (Paris: Gallimard, 1954), p. 188.

temporaneous set of essays covering the eight-year period ending in 1932. Once again there is evidence that Montherlant was looking at death as a natural phenomenon and that he discussed it in rational, courageous terms, forty years before he took his own life. Here is an excerpt:

> On a fait de la mort une chose trop importante. Elle est un point de maturité où la vie éclate, et tout est dans l'ordre...
>
> La mort est triste. Elle n'est pas odieuse... Il m'est impossible de me rebeller contre cette loi qu'il nous faut disparaître, d'autant moins insupportable que pas une fois elle ne s'est laissé violer (22).

Montherlant's attitude towards death differs from that of Camus and Ionesco, the other two leading contemporary writers on the theme. Whereas Ionesco fears it and Camus hates it, Montherlant welcomes it at times, accepts it at others. It is significant that the particular section just quoted, written in 1924, is entitled «Chant funèbre pour les morts de Verdun». A propos of his fund-raising for the *ossuaire,* the monument at Douaumont, he writes:

> Il y en a qui devant les ruines ont le réflexe: à quoi bon vivre? et nous parlent de la vanité des choses humaines. Leur sophisme oublie que le plaisir que nous donnons aux autres et à nous-mêmes a atteint son but, quoi qu'il arrive ensuite, et qu'ainsi, où il y eut une heure seulement de plaisir vrai, il ne peut pas y avoir de vanité. A plus forte raison soixante années, qu'il ne tient qu'à nous de remplir d'heures belles et bonnes, je ne puis pas dire sérieusement que cela n'est rien. «Ensuite, le

(22) *Mors et Vita, op. cit.,* p. 51.

néant.» Eh bien, va pour le néant. Les écoliers s'empoisonnent-ils leurs vacances parce qu'en octobre il faudra *rentrer*? Il n'y a pas là matière à soupirer, mais à prendre garde de ne pas perdre son temps (23).

In this elegy, Montherlant expresses gratitude for the great gift of life and a noble readiness to die at its end. Those men who forget or refuse to enjoy life are called impious. For himself, he claims that «le néant» will find him remembering the joys he has experienced and «plus reconnaissant de les avoir reçues, que révolté de me les voir ravies... Ce n'est pas la mort qui est le grand malheur, c'est la maladie» (24).

What is evil then —useless and inexplicable— is physical suffering, which spoils «la perspective de l'agonie». This quotation occurs in «Explicit mysterium», Montherlant's «Justification passionnée de la vie», wherein he states unequivocally that, without desiring or seeking death, he refuses to be horrified by it, for it is, after all, a natural event. «Les fleurs se fanent, les nuées se dissipent, chaque chose fait son temps et disparaît; les vivants sont perdus d'avance... Le tout est de mourir ayant suffisamment joui de la vie... Mais il arrive qu'un homme, dès trente ans, ait suffisamment joui de la vie» (25). As for after death, he said it made no difference to him whether he had Christian burial, cremation, «ou fosse commune, tout cela est égal. Il n'y a donc pas à demander l'une plutôt que l'autre dans un testament» (26). Forty

(23) *Ibid.*, p. 49.
(24) *Ibid.*, pp. 51-52.
(25) In *Mors et Vita*, pp. 125-127, *passim.*
(26) Ibid., p. 128. A propos of wills and testaments, there is another reference to their pointlessness in *La Petite Infante de*

years later, this usually consistent man did write such a testament, however, and he specifically requested cremation. In this statement of May 15, 1972, he also asked for several medical examinations to verify that he was really dead and he forebade any viewing of his corpse, any ceremony, flowers, wreaths, or orations (27). In explanation of why Montherlant changed his mind, it could be argued that he did not, but that, having no immediate family, he felt sure that friends or strangers would be more scrupulous and punctilious than relatives. What is beyond dispute is that Montherlant, throughout his life, reflected on death, whether natural, self-inflicted, or caused by war. The essays of the 1920's reveal his conviction that death was not the worst eventuality and that it was preferable to «une vie basse» (28). Therefore, it is entirely logical for Montherlant to accept even more firmly the notion of individual control of happiness.

Let us recall that Montherlant's list of works in which he discussed suicide began with *Aux fontaines du désir* and then mentioned «Un sens perdu» in *Service inutile* (29). The title of the essay refers to honor, itself no longer honored by contemporary

---

Castille (Paris: Bernard Grasset, 1929, p. 151), which constitutes the second volume of *Les Voyageurs traqués*: «... c'est la duperie suprême que d'exprimer des 'dernières volontés', puisqu'il est admis que vos héritiers, si elles choquent leurs principes, trouvent un biais pour ne pas les exécuter. Ils désobéissent à ce qu'un être, et que parfois ils 'aiment', leur a demandé dans l'heure la plus sacrée, et ils le font la conscience tranquille. Nous voyons ce cas tous les jours.»

(27) *Le Monde* (le 27 septembre 1972), p. 13.

(28) *Service inutile,* first published 1935, reprinted with *Mors et Vita, op. cit.*, p. 207.

(29) *Ibid.*, pp. 274-282. First published in *Le Jour,* 1933.

France. When a mayor's aide at Charolles is discovered to have been stealing food, he kills himself. A Japanese officer's wife commits suicide so that her husband will not have to worry about her when he is in battle. Society's reaction to both events disgusts Montherlant, who sees honor and sacrifice in these two cases. The most striking example, however, is that of Serge Dimitrief, the ex-Tsarist officer *cum* Parisian dishwasher. He jumped from a window as a sacrifice and expiation for the 1932 murder of President Doumer by a fellow Russian. «'Je meurs pour la France'», was the émigré's message of love to the country which had accepted him. Some Frenchmen commented that he killed himself to escape a life of misery, ascribing to his noble act motives of hypocrisy and insincerity. Montherlant, with respect for Dimitrief and loathing for such insensitivity on the part of his countrymen, accuses them of recognizing honor only in time of war.

The volume's last remaining reference to death and suicide appears in a 1933 speech at the Ecole supérieure de Guerre. Montherlant distinguishes between heroic suicides and those which are escapist. He mentions an officer in a last-ditch stand, blowing himself up, or a captain sinking with his vessel, or *hara-kiri* performed as a lesson for a pupil. These belong, it seems to me, to the category Durkheim considered altruistic suicides (30); what he called

(30) Emile Durkheim, *op. cit.*, pp. 233-242 *passim*, 260-262. Durkheim points out, however, that some cases of «suicide égoïste» might have equally moral bases, and that these types of suicide cannot be separated on moral grounds, for «... là où il met tellement haut la personnalité individuelle qu'il n'aperçoit plus aucune fin qui la dépasse, il la respecte chez les autres» (p. 263). To my mind, this position is one with which Montherlant would concur.

«Suicides égoïstes», acts for glory, are also praised by Montherlant at the War College. Recall the earlier text, «La Mort de Peregrinos», a suicide committed as a gesture. In his lecture, Montherlant speaks of similar acts «pour une raison mystique, dans une pensée de rachat». He approves the occasional answer by such a man: «'Parce que cela me plaît'. Et, en vérité, c'est bien cela, il se sacrifie pour le plaisir... Le plaisir d'atteindre à la réalisation absolue de soi-même et de la couronner de la façon la plus haute... C'est aussi le plaisir d'affirmer son indépendance à l'égard de la nature, en se substituant à elle» (31).

Pleasure, satisfaction, and gratification are all terms associated chiefly with sensuality. We have seen that Montherlant elevates the senses above the mind; therefore, it is logical for him to choose acts that are personally attractive rather than those that are preached by religion, law, or society. The creative artist, according to Montherlant, must especially be independent, and so a writer may, without despair, consciously and calmly decide to end a life no longer productive. As has been illustrated by Montherlant's own pronouncements, suicide is a welcome and respectable recourse for a man no longer capable of sensual pleasure, especially when he happens to be an artist no longer at the peak of his aesthetic achievement (32).

---

(31) *Service inutile, op. cit.*, pp. 284-286.

(32) However, in reviewing *Mais aimons-nous ceux que nous aimons?*, A. G. Branan says Montherlant was «in full possession of his literary talent until the very end» (*French Review*, XLVIII (March 1975), 801.

ATTITUDES ON DEATH: TIME PERSPECTIVE

As an old man, Montherlant found increasing disabilities, but out of long-standing pride, avoided displaying them. Martine Cadieu tells of the last time they dined together, when he refused to let her come to escort him to the restaurant. His visual impairment had made descending a staircase a painful procedure he did not wish her to witness. He showed her the vial of cyanide that he always carried, for his ultimate decision was to be ever-ready. He managed to laugh and yet they were speaking of death:

> Nous parlons de la mort comme de l'amour, comme de vivre, écrire, regarder en face. Je ne sais plus —je n'ai jamais rien noté— combien de fois nous avons évoqué le suicide,... Aussi simplement de la mort que de tout le reste et avec la même franchise... (1).

It must be noted that what is lucid, sensible, courageous, and realistic in a man of seventy-six seems a morbid preoccupation in a man of thirty-three. Let us flashback to what he wrote in an essay entitled «Le Dernier retour»:

---

(1) «Montherlant, l'ami», *Nouvelle Revue Française* (février 1973), pp. 24-25.

> Un homme meurt, pendant que les domestiques et la garde volent ses objets, et son meilleur ami ses notes intimes, pour les tripatouiller. Il a demandé à ne recevoir pas les sacrements; on les lui a donnés, de force. Il a demandé à être porté tout droit du lit funéraire à la fosse commune; on lui fait un enterrement religieux. Il y a dix personnes à cet enterrement, et trois au cimetière. Cet homme c'est moi, dans quelques années (2).

Although this third volume of *Les Voyageurs traqués* does not deal with suicide, it is extremely rich as an account of flight, disenchantment, and pessimism—three personal states that sometimes lead to despairing suicide, a type quite unlike Montherlant's own act of 1972. Even travel was not a pleasure in that mood. He questioned the purpose or value of love, adventure, freedom, and even expressed an atypical «manque de désir... Je suis arrivé à la limite de ce que je pouvais dans le sens de vivre (j'entends: vivre ardemment), au point où il faut tout changer. Je ferme la vie comme on ferme un livre. Je ferme ce temps où j'ai été moins heureux dans la liberté que je ne le fus un jour dans la contrainte...» (pp. 159-160). The tone gets more and more despairing, more and more nihilistic, as he calls himself the brother of two other exiles, Seneca and Ovid. He questions what it is that is dragging him eternally onward in his flight and finds only himself and no justification (pp. 186-187). He describes his joyless state which neither work nor

---

(2) *Un Voyageur solitaire est un Diable* (Paris: Gallimard, 1961), p. 169. Further quotations from this volume will be documented parenthetically in the text. Mostly written between 1925 and 1929, originally published 1945, the book, according to Montherlant (p. 179), takes its title from Mohammed.

pleasure affects. His vocabulary includes several significant repetitions: «Pour rien», «silence», and «A quoi bon...?» (pp. 187-188).

Attempting a more systematic study of Montherlant's attitudes towards death, we note that, in addition to the persona of such essays of youth as *Aux fontaines du désir* and *Mors et Vita* (treated in the preceding chapter), there are fictional expressions of the reactions of young people to the death of others. One of Montherlant's novelistic characters is Alban de Bricoule, the thoughtful soldier of *Le Songe* (1922) and the adolescent who grows up in *Les Garçons* (1969). A third example of the attitude of young people towards death can be seen in *Le Chaos et la nuit,* both in Pascualita's relationship with her father and how he thinks she regards him in old age.

In *Le Songe,* the theme of death is highlighted beginning with chapter VII of Part I. War uplifts, exalts, and excites Alban. He seems to thrive on danger, and it whets his appetite for making love and procreating (3). He tells Dominique when she visits him at the front that people exaggerate the sorrow of death. He envisages it as a reunion with Marcus Aurelius, and he sees himself ready to die after having experienced happiness. However, his deep affection for Prinet keeps him from imagining his comrade's death (4). There is a striking scene of the death of a German soldier, weeping while Alban, initially gentle with this pitiful enemy, wrests his hand from the boy's grasp (5). Montherlant masterfully evokes, in this

---

(3) In *Romans* (Paris: Bibliothèque de la Pléiade, 1959), pp. 76-78.
(4) *Ibid.,* pp. 89-90.
(5) *Ibid.,* pp. 146-147.

early novel, the intense agitation of a young man in love with war, trembling to think he may die with the weaklings rather than in communion with Prinet. Alban would like to die viewed as a hero by his comrade (6), but it is Prinet who dies, far from his presence (7). And with that death, Alban's attitude towards heroism and his adoration of war come to a final point that is flat, undramatic, but esthetically perfect (8).

Towards the end of *Les Garçons* (9), the mother of Alban de Bricoule is dying. She is only in her early forties, but she has a fatal case of tuberculosis. She loses interest in her son and her admirer, and no one writes to her. Her son goes to balls and out to meet ladies of easy virtue. His mother, a proud woman, does not ask him to forego any pleasure, and indeed she seems no longer to care even for him. Montherlant describes her dying in a probing, psychological way that is of special interest since Mme de Bricoule, like the hero of *Le Chaos et la nuit,* is complex, isolated, and noble: three characteristics also possessed by the novelist. An especially rich sentence wholly consistent with Montherlant's basic philosophy is this observation about Mme de Bricoule's apathy: «Nous mourons quand il n'y a plus personne pour qui nous voulions vivre» (p. 335). But to see the attitude of youth towards death is to look rather at how Alban views his mother's consumptive dying.

---

(6) *Ibid.,* p. 149.
(7) *Ibid.,* p. 163.
(8) *Ibid.,* p. 173.
(9) (Paris: Gallimard, 1969). Page references will accompany the quotations, parenthetically, hereafter.

Although Alban usually seems calm, he does cry as he carries out his mother's request that her letters be thrown into the Seine. «A sept jours de sa mort, il s'éveillait enfin: il se mettait à l'aimer quand elle ne l'aimait plus.» He recognizes how broad-minded and unconventional she has been in raising him; furthermore, she has never bored him (p. 343)! He wants her not to die, but it is «too late» (p. 344). After her death, Alban weeps and realizes he didn't cry when the separation from his beloved Serge occurred. The supposition is that his tears for his mother are formed from a combination of the two griefs (p. 345). He even dreams that his mother and Serge ignore or do not see him, and he recognizes that, without ever having met Serge, Mme de Bricoule loved him (pp. 352-353).

Another example of filial reaction to death is Pascualita's. Actually her father's interpretation is more important, since her rôle in *Le Chaos et la nuit* is inferior to his. In Part I, the only interesting reaction discernible in Pascualita is her reference to «la pièce sacrée», the nurse's room that is ready just in case her father falls terminally ill. His response is that the room is for his fiancée, who is not *l'infirmière* but *la mort* (10). Although, in truth, his daughter does not want his death, he has the recurrent thought, «'Il nous embête avec sa mort'» (pp. 176, 180, 182, 270). It serves as a leit-motiv, and it shows what he thinks Pascualita may be thinking.

In any case, she does not follow his last wishes. As has been noted, Montherlant's non-fiction makes

---

(10) (Paris: Gallimard, 1963), p. 125. Further references to *Le Chaos et la nuit* will occur parenthetically in the text.

references to this familial disrespect for last wishes, and here we see the same opinion espoused in a novel. There is a funeral service; the paper says Celestino received the last sacrament, and the tombstone erected indicates that God is praised (pp. 279-280). Obviously, Pascualita as next of kin, albeit influenced by her conservative uncle, is the person responsible.

* * *

From death viewed by the young Alban in war, Alban and his mother, Pascualita, and of course the direct expression by the essayist Montherlant in his twenties and thirties —let us proceed to a second section on death. How is it viewed by mature characters, and how did the author himself express his opinions in essays during his forties? In the preceding chapter, we have already considered the latter by examining his notebooks. Yet there are two remarks that were not discussed. The mature Montherlant, looking at elderly people, expressed sympathy and understanding, as well as the view that the choice must be between suicide or an acceptance of diminishing powers. Montherlant denies that F..., a man of sixty-eight, is really living, underlining the word and adding: «Spectacle sinistre» (11).

The other remark is focussed on the alternative: a lucid old man discovers that the remainder of life, instead of being the pinnacle «de conduite, quelque chose de tellement riche et plein, est gouverné par le hasard, l'absurdité et le désoeuvrement». Heroically

---

(11) *Carnets: Années 1930 à 1944*, 22e éd. (Paris: Gallimard, 1957), p. 393.

he kills himself to break free from this diminished existence «plus tôt» (12).

Overlapping the dates of this collection of notes is another book of Montherlant's thoughts during the Occupation. Although he was only forty-six or forty-seven, he seems preoccupied by the theme of death. In this instance, war rather than old age produced the reaction. He imagines a future time when he will be too ill and weak to reach from his bed to a pair of scissors lying on a table (13). He comments on the beneficial effects of indifference to death (14), an attitude quite in line with his love of Rome and the Stoïcs. Fear of death is a horrible thing, he feels, but he has never «souri d'un homme qui avait peur de la mort» (15).

Bearing some resemblance to the Stoics, Madame de Bricoule in *Les Garçons* sets out consciously to prepare for Death. Actually, quite altruistically, she arranges for Alban to disengage himself from her, so that he will have an easier adjustment later:

> Elle le mettait à la porte, ou tout comme. Elle évitait de poser son regard sur lui, évitait de regarder ce qu'elle avait le plus chéri en ce monde, au bord de ne le plus voir pour jamais. Ainsi s'avançait-elle, cadenassée et chancelante, jusqu'au bord de l'épouvantable aventure de mourir.
>
> Elle avait décidé qu'elle ne le ferait pas appeler, au moment qu'elle expirerait. Elle décida qu'il ne dînerait plus dans sa chambre à elle, auprès de son lit... Il y a sans doute un art de parler avec les

---

(12) *Ibid.*, p. 387.

(13) *Carnets XLII et XLIII: Du 1er Janvier 1942 au 31 Décembre 1943* (Paris: La Table ronde, 1948), p. 22.

(14) *Ibid.*, p. 61.

(15) *Ibid.*, p. 102.

> moribonds, mais cet art n'est pas dans les cordes des garçons de dix-huit ans. Et de qui est-il dans les cordes? Il n'y a pas de langage commun entre celui qui va mourir et celui qui va vivre (p. 337).

The language barrier is not the result of a generation gap; it stems from a wider gulf: the living vs. the dying. The relatives who come unannounced are people she cannot bear —boors who actually think she looks well. Since Montherlant is not a believer, he can use Jesus metaphorically with no fear of blasphemy: Madame de Bricoule is compared in her loneliness to Jesus, who is called «le supérieur» (pp. 340-341). She tells Alban that she is ashamed of dying, as if it were obscene (p. 342). Actually, Montherlant steps in rather directly and plays the part of omniscient narrator. He describes why the cousins came —not for Alban, not for his mother, but to please socially-prominent Uncle Edouard. Montherlant's cynicism, which seems as perspicacious for America as for Europe, extends to these upper-class types; his snobbery is not one of class. On the other hand, the dying person commands his respect and understanding in the same measure that the relatives command his disgust; the reason is not the dying but the character and quality of Madame de Bricoule. The narrator directly quotes those who accuse the victim of mistaken judgment in selecting physicians on her own. «Mme de Bricoule n'est pas une morte fraîche, elle est une accusée. Elle a d'ailleurs été toujours une accusée, pour la famille. Et puis, l'accusée vous permet de vous en fiche, et de ne pas le cacher» (p. 345).

In this book in another case, Montherlant's irony comes out strikingly, but it is an older character, the

Abbé de Pradts, the demonic figure of the play, *La Ville dont le prince est un enfant.* At the very end of *Les Garçons* (pp. 370-372), he undergoes a religious conversion. He is influenced by the simple faith of a seventy-year-old Polish housekeeper. He takes extreme unction, and Montherlant punctures the balloon of the pious by his dry wit: «... et il cessa d'être. C'était le 7 mai de 1940. Dieu rappelait à lui l'abbé de Pradts juste à temps pour qu'il ne fût pas collaborateur» (p. 372).

Not wit but virtuosity of a different nature is displayed in *Un Assassin est mon maître,* a psychoanalytical case study of a paranoid. At times pitiful, at times ridiculous, Exupère, this dazzling example of Montherlant's late fiction, commits a kind of suicide. He does not pull a trigger or swallow cyanide as the author was to do, but he is responsible for his own death by starvation and neglect. The most fascinating aspect of the case is that he reaches out to the real writer, pleading to be saved, but his letters asking for money never have return addresses so that no help can ever be administered (16). The sense of guilt, the obsession, the compulsions can be removed or relieved only by cessation of life. The death-wish underlies the inordinate fear in this particular man. It is clear, however, that he is not an average man; perhaps he cannot then be taken as an example of a mature character expressing typical views. Yet the fact that Montherlant focusses on him, minutely painting his psychological portrait down to the most ignominious details, gives us the right to examine

(16) (Paris: Gallimard, 1971), pp. 229-231.

his preoccupation with death and his relation to Montherlant and the theme of suicide. Indeed, this novel even makes two overt references to the theme. For example, «... celui qui va se suicider ne pourrait donner les raisons de son suicide, elles aussi trop diverses et intriquées; s'il donne des raisons, elles sont élémentaires, et ne recouvrent pas la vérité» (17). Often, trivial factors enter into fatal actions: «Combien de types, se suicidant —*et non pas du tout pour une question d'argent, tout au plus pour une question où l'argent joue un tout petit rôle,*— ne l'auraient pas fait s'ils avaient reçu à l'instant fatal un gros chèque!» (18). This remark shows cynicism but perspicacity and is not so different from Camus' point that, despite a man's having been worn away by five years of bereavement, his suicide can be precipitated one day when a friend speaks to him «sur un ton indifférent» (19). In all events, *Un Assassin est mon maître* contributes doubly to our investigation, since its mentally ill hero is a person of mature years, while the perceptive author is an aged Montherlant.

Turning squarely to the aged and their attitudes towards death, it has been shown that Montherlant drew a satirical sketch of the Abbé de Pradts in *Les Garçons.* There was, however, no joking about age. That has always been a subject that evoked compassion in Montherlant, even when he himself was in the prime of life (20). His masterly conception of that man of

(17) *Ibid.*, p. 134.
(18) *Ibid.*, p. 223.
(19) Albert Camus, *Le Mythe de Sisyphe* (Paris: Collection Idées-Gallimard, 1942 [1966]), p. 17.
(20) In his *Carnets XXII à XXVIII: Du 23 Avril 1932 au 22 Novembre 1934* [actually goes to 17 février 1935] (Paris: La Table ronde, 1955), Montherlant mentions two signs of aging in people:

ambiguities, the Portuguese king Ferrante; his finely etched Cardinal of Spain, a very aged figure; the heroic suicide of Persilès in *Brocéliande*; the rueful portrayal of an old, seemingly grotesque Don Juan; the pitiful spinster of advanced years in *Celles qu'on prend dans ses bras* —are ample pieces of evidence that Montherlant never failed to take seriously the whole proposition of human senescence. And why? Undoubtedly the explanation lies in the question of death, the inevitable and absolute end. It is especially pertinent to our inquiry to look at some of his statements of the last years he lived —statements that he set down in his own name in notebooks and essays.

Comparing his literary disdain of public opinion to his decision not to be upset by the thought of death, he adds: «Je ne vais quand même pas perdre mon temps à regretter de devoir mourir (11 septembre 1971)» (21). This calm acceptance of the disagreeable fact of death appears clearly in a book also written during Montherlant's later life, although earlier than *La Marée du soir*. He records, in *Va jouer avec cette poussière*, the disproportion between topical problems and *la condition humaine*. Although he calls death for each individual the most absolute of catastrophes, he adds, like a Roman philosopher: «Cependant il est contraire à la raison de ne pas s'accommoder à un

when they find days very long and when they start being kind to the aged on buses and in the subway (p. 172). He also shows deep respect for such people as a retired colonel, who is given a cot in his children's living-room when formerly he commanded three thousand men (p. 190).

(21) *La Marée du soir: Carnets 1968-1971* (Paris: Gallimard, 1972), p. 150.

destin fatal. C'est même dans notre mort, je crois, plus que nulle part ailleurs, que nous devrions, s'il se pouvait, mettre une pointe de désinvolture» (22). He faces the fact that when we die, all our perceptions die as well, but he calls it absurd to suffer «pour un petit point d'une petite molécule... Il n'est pas possible que nous mourions en donnant l'impression que nous avons pris une petite molécule tout à fait au sérieux. Il m'est assez indifférent de me perdre. Ce à quoi je tiens, c'est à me perdre sans illusions (19 septembre 1964)». He adds that like the Stoics, he has «loved the inevitable» (23). It would appear that he also shares with Voltaire the recognition that man is not as great as he thinks and that it is foolish to hope to live beyond what is possible for a human being (24). If death is natural, one can say that man must wish «'ce que veut l'ordre des choses'». Yet, a person who commits suicide is also understandable, since it is human to «'vouloir se libérer de l'ordre des choses'». Likewise, «Si on est tué: 'Comment n'était-ce pas arrivé plus tôt?'» (25). In other words, Montherlant is not easily shocked by any kind of death.

At first blush, nothing seems more of a contrast to these notebook entries than the point of view of a fictional character in one of Montherlant's finest works. If we bear always uppermost in our minds the motto «Syncrétisme et alternance», it does not seem so strange that the Stoical writer could so vividly

(22) *Carnets 1958-1964* (Paris: Gallimard, 1966), pp. 185-186.

(23) *Ibid.*, p. 187.

(24) Voltaire, *Micromégas* in *Romans, Contes et Mélanges,* 2 vol. (Paris: Livre de Poche, 1972), I, 44 and 37.

(25) *Va jouer avec cette poussière* (Paris: Gallimard, 1966), p. 149.

describe a man beset by old age and approaching death. Celestino in *Le Chaos et la nuit* is a complex protagonist, as so many of Montherlant's dramatic ones have been. In novels, however, there tends to be a confusion between the narrator and the author. Near the end of Part One, an omniscient narrator comments on the transformation wrought upon Celestino by old age:

> La réalité était devenue pour lui un autre monde: son véritable monde était celui de la mort... Et toujours il en revenait à la même interrogation: «Comment mourir? Comment se comporter en arrivant en vue de la mort?»... Blague la philosophie. Blague, bien sûr, blague des blagues la religion (26).

Then the narrator, thinking out loud, wonders why modern times, precisely since the nineteenth century, have made men so fearful of death. «Est-ce qu'on n'avait peur de la mort que depuis qu'on ne croyait plus en Dieu?» (p. 117). Celestino prepares a will specifying that his body should be cremated without any religious rites (pp. 120-121). Although no decent critic should jump to conclusions linking authors and their characters, one must admit that it is no mere coincidence that Montherlant should write such a testament of last wishes (see page 34). Part of the strength of this particular novel is the way Celestino is brought close to the reader, almost as if the author were after all more involved than usual. In describing Celestino's reflections upon French attitudes towards

(26) (Paris: Gallimard, 1963), p. 116. Further quotations from *Le Chaos et la nuit* will be documented parenthetically in the text.

death and old age —reflections that contrast his own consciousness of the inevitable link between the two phenomena and the French refusal to face the ugly truth, Montherlant makes the reader side with the protagonist: «Lui, il jugeait que c'est un vieillard qui ne pense pas à la mort qui est un malade: sa maladie s'appelle l'*inconscience*» (pp. 123-124). In other words, Celestino is made more intelligent, more honest, and more human than most people. Montherlant's lifelong admiration for Spain fits nicely with the way Celestino, although an exile for years in France, has retained his Spanish qualities.

Part Two opens with Celestino's preparations to return to Spain, following receipt of the news that his sister has died in Madrid. He is convinced that he too will die in Spain and that his death there will be an enactment of destiny:

> —Mourir exilé, c'est bien. Mourir en prison, c'est mieux. Mourir assassiné ou fusillé ou suicidé, c'est mieux encore. Je pars pour accomplir un destin que je n'avais pas accompli jusqu'au bout. Je pars pour mourir en homme de mon époque (p. 150).

The first three sentences of this quotation do not appear so different after all from the statement in *Va jouer avec cette poussière* (see pp. 47-48). It becomes evident that *Le Chaos et la nuit* is Montherlant's most detailed treatment of death and old age, but it is not as clearly gloomy as the essays of the young Montherlant. Celestino is still a *voyageur traqué,* but he ultimately succeeds in facing death heroically. Montherlant's irony is turned on Pascualita, who is proven wrong about her father. What seemed to her his inordinate fear of returning to Franco Spain is shown to be a correct judgment. The reader empathizes with Celestino, who is superior intellectually and morally (in the political and social spheres) to his daughter and brother-in-law. It can be observed then that Montherlant, not only in his notebooks and essays of old age, but also in his fictional expression of the same years, possesses a lucidity and an awareness of reality that are remarkably Stoic. He remains clear-headed, capable of rational evaluation, and very pagan.

At the beginning of chapter VI, the Gare d'Austerlitz appears to Celestino as the station from whence he will go to death, just as French soldiers felt about the Gare du Nord and the Gare de l'Est (p. 174). He names his native land «le pays de la peur», but he decides that it is not he but his old age that is afraid (pp. 175-176). Old age is also blamed for his belated love of money (p. 135), a new preoccupation that seems to him a betrayal of the working class (p. 196). Strangely enough, once the border is crossed at Irun, his fear vanishes (p. 183). Instead, in the streets of Madrid, he is conscious of a special «art» of living: «y tuer et n'y être pas tué». That art is named «Tauromachie» (p. 190), a term that has always been dear to Montherlant the amateur bull-fighter.

Another seeming connection between Celestino and his creator occurs in a description of a fire burning in a brazier in a small bar in Madrid: «... et maintenant il comprenait pourquoi ce feu l'avait arrêté: parce que c'était un feu pareil à celui qui le consumerait lui-même, au Père Lachaise, un jour prochain» (p. 203). Actually, that will be the final destination of the *voyageur traqué*. If the novel indeed illustrates Montherlant's attitude towards death and senescence, it is significant that Celestino's awareness of an approaching cremation «lui était plutôt agréable» (p. 203). As time goes on, he even toys with the notion of purposely catching cold, since he recognizes: «Tout est sans issue, fors une seule issue, qui est de cesser d'être». However, he would rather die, he decides, in Paris (p. 224). Soon it is not death that is a frightening thought but what would precede: prison or torture if he were to be arrested, what he understatedly calls «l'avant-mort et des conditions matérielles qui l'accompagneraient» (pp. 227-228). He begins to identify with bulls in a brilliant passage, Pascalian in theme and style —a series of antitheses, culminating in a pithy summation:

> De plus en plus défiant et de plus en plus dupé, de plus en plus méchant et de plus en plus bafoué, de plus en plus ensemble impuissant et dangereux, voué à la mort inéluctable et capable encore cependant de mettre à mort: tel était le taureau à la fin de sa vie, et tel l'homme (p. 254).

He cannot stand to watch the *peones* kicking the bull to make him fall, or the bull lashing out at them but dying nonetheless, much to the amusement of the men (pp. 256-258). Spain is no longer Celestino's country (p. 261). What does any country, any social system, any war matter, in comparison to the overpowering knowledge of his imminent death? Formerly thought of in the abstract, now unmistakably real and concrete, the existential fact is all that counts (p. 267). In a description that seems appropriate for Montherlant himself, Celestino is «Seul pour le face à face avec la mort... Et ce *fuera todos!* n'était rien d'autre que sa vieille passion de faire le vide autour de lui, arrivée enfin à l'absolu et au parfait». As he is stricken, «Il eut la certitude de sa mort, de sa mort peut-être dans cet instant même, et en fut satisfait. La mort était la seule chose qui fût importante, et pourtant, elle aussi, elle était indifférente» (p. 269).

If we concede that some facets of an author's personality or philosophy may be distributed among different fictional characters, it seems reasonable that Celestino should express Montherlant's conception of senescence in a more authentic way than the old bachelors of *Les Célibataires,* a novel of Montherlant's maturity. We can conclude that, beyond the normal fear, pain, and struggle associated with death, it remains the greatest of paradoxes. Death is so important, so unique that all else pales by comparison, and yet, in itself, it is acceptable, in Montherlant's view. That is to say that *la mort* is so normal a thing, so inevitable, that one must do «ce qu'il y avait à faire avec elle, correctement» (p. 269). The quality of personal courage and nobility, of Hispanic honor, has always been revered by Henry de Montherlant.

AEDIFICABO ET DESTRUAM

During an interview that probably occurred around 1965, Henry de Montherlant said to Gilbert Ganne: «J'ai eu une vie exceptionnellement heureuse» (1). This summation seems proof positive against those students of Montherlant who see him as despairing and pessimistic. Better adjectives for his attitude would be «nihilistic» and «skeptical», which do not necessarily reflect gloomy states of mind or soul. For example, the mature Montherlant of the 1930's already empathized with elderly people, those who were maltreated by their families and who hanged themselves in order to escape from the cruelty of relatives (2). Yet he was not wallowing in sadness; his conception of life was unsentimental and sophisticated, but neither unprincipled nor apathetic. Resembling the Camusian opinion that the cause for which a man may be willing to die is often the reason he wishes to live (3), Montherlant juxtaposes two

(1) Gilbert Ganne, *Interviews impubliables* (Paris: Plon, 1965), p. 179.

(2) *Carnets XXII à XXVIII:* Du 23 Avril 1932 au 22 novembre 1934 [actually continues until Feb. 17, 1935] (Paris: La Table ronde, 1955), pp. 13-14, 72-73.

(3) Albert Camus, *Le Mythe de Sisyphe* (Paris: Collection Idées, Gallimard, 1942 [1966]), p. 16.

states of mind: readiness to risk one's life and adoration of life itself. The very willingness to risk death can be understood «comme une façon de donner du ton à la vie» (4). He refused to believe in so-called ideals, saying: «Je ne crois pas à ce genre de choses (les idéaux), et souvent je désire mourir, pour ne plus voir les gens qui y croient, tant ils m'ennuient» (5). This expression of Montherlant's distaste surprisingly resembles Roquentin's disgust with the self-proclaimed and misnamed «humanists» (6). Montherlant's attack on abstraction parallels that of Sartre, and it is significant that the dates of composition are approximately contemporaneous. Like the existentialists, Montherlant emphasizes the concrete, particularly when he records his passionate opposition to «Les serins qui disent que la vie 'n'a pas de sens', quand il y a toujours la possibilité de rendre heureux ce qu'on aime, et de se nourrir de son bonheur du même coup» (7).

A final illustration from the same notebooks is Montherlant's assertion that, more than anyone can know, he has been «comblé». He requests that those who may in future visit his deathbed be especially aware of the gifts he has had from life (8). Even some of Montherlant's more sombre essays betray glimmers of brightness. Typical of Montherlant are the seeming paradoxes, the states alternating between creation and

---

(4) Entry for February 8, 1934 in Montherlant's *Carnets XXII à XXVIII*, p. 109.

(5) *Ibíd.*, p. 195.

(6) Jean-Paul Sartre, *La Nausée* (Paris: Livre de Poche Université, 1938 [1966]), pp. 165-166.

(7) *Carnets XXII à XXVIII*, pp. 213-214.

(8) *Ibíd.*, p. 216.

destruction, glorification of life but acceptance of death. In *Aux fontaines du désir*, already seen to contain more than one evocation of suicide, there also occurs a lyrical appreciation of natural beauty. After a passage of profound disgust with some of the crassness and cheapness abroad in the world, Montherlant exclaims: «... je supplie qu'on me permette de ne plus désirer, et de me préparer au pelottement du grand sommeil hivernal, en attendant que l'odeur d'un jasmin me ressuscite» (9).

An affirmative tone within a nihilistic framework marks the ending of «Explicit mysterium», an essay already cited in connection with the theme of suicide. Therein, Montherlant very lyrically apostrophizes a «Monde sans Dieu, monde sans justice finale, —monde sans lois, monde sans volonté—» free of shadows or mists, a world he deems worthy of man (10). In that same essay, he criticizes «le culte des Morts», insisting that the mere state of death should not in itself convey honor in inferior men. Only talent and virtue should command respect (11).

These high standards are in accord with the conception of life and death enunciated by Maurice Barrès, one of the French writers that Montherlant admired, though not uncritically (12). Barrès shares with Montherlant not only an inordinate propensity for individualism but also an emphasis on Stoical

---

(9) *Aux fontaines du désir* (Paris: Bernard Grasset, 1927), p. 234.

(10) *Mors et Vita*, reprinted with *Service inutile* (Paris: Gallimard, 1954), p. 133.

(11) *Ibid.*, p. 126.

(12) See «Barrès s'éloigne», in *Aux fontaines du désir*, pp. 85-143.

acceptance of human mortality and the notion of nothingness (13). They also share an intense appreciation of eroticism. Long before Montherlant, Barrès elevated sensuality above intellectuality, as the following quotation shows: «Observer, prendre des notes, les rassembler systématiquement, toute cette froide compréhension par l'extérieur nous mène moins loin que ne feraient cinq minutes d'amour. Nous ne pénétrons le secret des âmes que dans l'ivresse de partager leurs passions mêmes» (14). As Jean d'Ormesson points out in the finest of all the necrological tributes to Montherlant, Barrès should be recognized today less as a chauvinist and more as a sybarite: «le Barrès du culte du moi et *Du sang, de la volupté et de la mort*» (15). He explains Montherlant's suicide in what appears to me the most intelligent way when he refers to the shock it evoked, despite its predictability. (I suppose that most people believe that truth is stranger than fiction.) D'Ormesson repeats the list that Montherlant gave (see above, page 23) of seven works honoring suicide and then adds *La Marée du soir*. «Huit livres où le suicide

---

(13) Maurice Barrès, *Du sang, de la volupté et de la mort* (Paris: Albert Fontemoing, 1903), p. 13 (Introduction), p. 56, pp. 78-79. First published 1894.

(14) *Ibíd.*, p. 306.

(15) «L'équinoxe de septembre», *Nouvelle Revue Française* (février 1973), p. 45. Further quotations from this article, whose title recalls Montherlant's book (Paris: Bernard Grasset, 1938), will be documented parenthetically in the text. Marcel Lobet, «Le suprême exil de Montherlant», *Revue générale*, n.º 8 (octobre 1972), p. 89, points out that Montherlant seems to have chosen the date, and even the hour, 4 P. M., on purpose. Lobet gives approaching blindness as the cause and mentions Nerval and especially Hemingway. Since Montherlant was not mentally ill, I find this comparison fallacious (see above, page 10), but the remark about the choice of day and hour has merit.

tient une place essentielle et où il est, non pas pardonné, mais toujours exalté» (p. 40).

In honoring suicide, Montherlant distinguished, says d'Ormesson, between «le suicide par protestation», and

> suicide sur ordre à la façon romaine... Il avait volontiers vu lui-même dans le suicide idéal comme un refus du monde et son allure qu'a refusé Montherlant. C'est lui-même et son vieillissement. La première stupeur passée, c'est évidemment là-dessus que plusieurs, et notamment les catholiques, se sont mis à l'attaquer. La grandeur et le courage n'auraient pas été du côté du refus d'un combat perdu, mais de son acceptation. C'est parce qu'il était vieux et qu'il devenait aveugle que Montherlant s'est tué. Je ne crois pas, en effet, qu'il y ait d'autre motif à sa décision. Mais comment faut-il la comprendre? (p. 44).

D'Ormesson's article is impressive precisely because he goes beyond the precipitating factors of blindness and old age to add the underlying explanation, which happens to be my own conviction as well —that Montherlant's suicide stemmed not from despair but from an appreciation of the true meaning of life.

> Barrès évoque dans *Amori et dolori sacrum* 'l'éternel motif de la mort par excès d'amour de la vie'. C'est à ce Barrès-là plus encore qu'aux Romains que se rattache, je crois, le Montherlant du suicide. Toute sa vie, c'est un lieu commun, Montherlant a été déchiré entre le bonheur et l'honneur, entre le plaisir et la grandeur... Lorsque l'âge et la maladie ont interdit le plaisir, la volupté, le bonheur, l'issue était toute trouvée... Oui, c'est bien 'l'éternel motif de la mort par excès d'amour de la vie' que je vois d'abord dans le suicide de

> Montherlant. Puisqu'il n'y avait plus rien à tirer de ce monde, mieux valait le quitter dans un dernier geste de panache (p. 46).

D'Ormesson stresses Montherlant's love of «le plaisir» as the best explanation of why he chose to die when life could no longer furnish him with such satisfactions (p. 47). Suicide, a solution pre-eminently Roman, is the act that best fuses «le culte de la grandeur et le goût du plaisir» (p. 48). D'Ormesson notes that with the exception of Catholics who were terribly disappointed by Montherlant's act, most people could see it as consistent and fitting. D'Ormesson alludes to Bergson's contention that «toute l'oeuvre d'un artiste ou d'un philosophe pouvait toujours se résumer en un point central d'où découlait l'ensemble de ses aspects les plus différents. Je ne suis pas sûr que pour Montherlant, ce point central —et rétrospectif— ne soit pas son suicide... La vie, la mort et l'oeuvre se justifient mutuellement» (p. 49).

In that same issue of the *Nouvelle Revue Française* devoted to Montherlant, Pierre Kyria stresses the problem of blindness, revealing that in May 1971, four months before his suicide, Montherlant was discouraged by his ill-health: «il y avait dans son angoisse une sorte de détermination amère qui gênait». But several days later, he apologized in writing, explaining the supremacy of physical suffering (16). It seems to me that Montherlant recognized that the only way to avoid pitying himself and asking others for compassion was to eliminate the sufferer. Years

(16) (Février 1973), pp. 30-31. The title is «Montherlant, une fidélité à l'exigence».

earlier, in «Chant funèbre», he had written that were he to go blind, he would bear up well: «'Je me dispersais, me dirais-je, dans un monde trop riche. Une partie m'en est dérobée. Ainsi, je vais pouvoir connaître à fond le reste'» (17). By way of understanding Montherlant's seeming inconsistency, let us note that his subsequent blindness was accompanied by old age and that by committing suicide he was sparing his friends from having to care for him. It seems obvious that Montherlant's handicaps played a rôle in his decision to kill himself, but that he came to that decision in a lucid, calm, and rational way.

In expressing to Renauld-Krantz his disgust with his own period, his horror of sinking into «une pourriture grandissante», he said he ought to have died earlier, before being subjected, in an enfeebled condition, to an «ignoble» world. The significant point for me is the description of Montherlant's tone: «grave certes, mais sans aucune lamentation dans la voix, détaché, serein» (18). Even the articles which stress his physical infirmity show him to be, at the time of his suicide, mentally sure and sound. Indeed, much of his writing during his last years indicates his clear-headedness as he thought of death and the value of choosing the hour himself.

In 1970, Montherlant writes sarcastically of society's hypocritical insistence that people who commit suicide should do so in a deceptive way: «Pas de revolver, quelle horreur! Pas même de cyanure,

---

(17) *Mors et vita,* reprinted with *Service inutile* (Paris: Gallimard, 1954), p. 51.

(18) *Nouvelle Revue Française* (février 1973), p. 19. The title of the article is «Le Chevalier du néant».

dépassé. Un nouveau poison, qui arrête le coeur... Le médecin peut parler d'infarctus. La décence sociale est sauve» (19). In almost a detached tone, the next year, Montherlant quotes Seneca on our fundamental right to «'la mort qui nous plaît'» (p. 136) and entertainingly records his youthful desire to die during sexual intercourse. However, as an elderly person, he imagines the plight of «la jeune personne prisonnière entre mes membres raidis, si j'avais une attaque (mort de Félix Faure, etc.), et je me suis efforcé d'éviter ce que je souhaitais auparavant» (p. 136). In the scale of «pleasant» deaths, the next best would be suicide, but, claims Montherlant, he would not try it because of legal dangers to any friend who would give him the *coup de grâce* (in the event he himself was unsuccessful) (20). To wind up this evaluation of «enjoyable» deaths, Montherlant mentions Petronius' choice: death while uttering obscenities (p. 137).

In a book published posthumously (21), Montherlant speaks of a doctor who had once obtained a medical furlough for him: «Quand les Allemands entrèrent dans Paris, en 1940, le docteur de Martel se suicida. La bêtise et la bassesse qui accueillent tout suicide

---

(19) *La Marée du soir: Carnets 1968-1971* (Paris: Gallimard, 1972), p. 101. Further quotations from this volume will be documented parenthetically in the text.

(20) However, one year later, Montherlant did kill himself, taking care to involve no one else and to use both a gun and poison for greater chance of success. In this connection, note Durkheim's much earlier discussion: «D'après la jurisprudence la plus générale, le complice du suicide est poursuivi comme homicide. Il n'en serait pas ainsi si le suicide était considéré comme un acte moralement indifférent», in *Le Suicide* (Paris: Félix Alcan, 1930), p. 371.

(21) *Mais aimons-nous ceux que nous aimons?* (Paris: Gallimard, 1973). The title, except for the conjunction, «Mais», is a quotation from Maurice Clavel. Page references for this volume will appear parenthetically in the text.

déferlèrent sur le corps du docteur de Martel. On ricana, on dit qu'il était neurasthénique» (pp. 24-25). The book of reminiscences was written during Montherlant's last summer; page 218 bears the date «Juillet-août 1972». Perhaps the only other pertinent passage from this book is to be found in the footnote on page 195; it deals with the great toreador, Belmonte:

> Il ne put pas supporter d'avoir soixante-dix ans, et, quatre jours avant l'apparition du 7 dans sa vie, il se tua d'un coup de revolver. Depuis peu on avait remarqué sa douceur particulière envers tous, et qu'il avait fait des cadeaux à ses amis: détails qui se retrouvent dans la mort de Caton d'Utique.

The quotation is especially interesting since it has been claimed that Montherlant's serious interest in suicide can be dated from the 1950's, specifically from Juan Belmonte (22). As this study has demonstrated, even the young Montherlant was attuned to the fatal attraction of suicide. What is clear is that his consideration of this theme increases in later life. In his last books as we have seen, there are frequent allusions to suicide. To those who quickly seize on facile explanations, including those who pityingly point to Montherlant's age and near-blindness as uncomplicated reasons for his own self-destruction, there is a warning prepared by the author himself in a preface to one of his plays:

> Les motifs qui ont poussé un artiste à exécuter telle oeuvre d'art peuvent être aussi profondément

(22) This is the view expressed by André Blanc, *Montherlant: un pessimisme heureux* (Paris: Editions du Centurion, 1968), pp. 211-212.

> nécessaires et cependant aussi indiscernables, si l'artiste ne les révèle pas, que les motifs véritables d'un suicide, enfouis et à jamais perdus pour le monde quand le mort n'a pas expliqué son geste, ou quand l'explication n'en est pas évidente (23).

Let us examine an additional piece of evidence to substantiate the claim that at the very time he did kill himself, he was not sad, neurotic, and despairing. He had survived such a period when he was young and miserable, when he was the *voyageur traqué.* In *Mais aimons-nous ceux que nous aimons?* (p. 165), he refers to August as «le mois tragique de l'année, du moins pour moi. Je l'avais éprouvé deux fois déjà à cette époque [unspecified, but shortly after 1923, when he resumed bull-fighting following his grandmother's demise], et devais l'éprouver souvent au long de ma vie». It would appear that, far from being *caused* by special problems, what continued to affect Montherlant as it had in earlier years was a seasonal malaise (remember Durkheim's comments on daylight and intensity of social interaction) or what Unamuno called «the tragic sense of life».

Indeed, one of the precepts of existentialism is the awareness of being and nothingness. Written in 1926, «Les Voyageurs traqués» expressed the young Montherlant's desire to be killed by time, dissolved utterly into a dreamless and final nothingness. Already as a young man, Montherlant was reflecting on metaphysics and finding «un ciel vide». Instead of being full of despair, however, he lucidly examined the notion and found it comforting, whether in moments

---

(23) See *Brocéliande,* suivi de *L'Art et la vie,* 2e édition (Paris: Gallimard, 1956), p. 9.

of pride or «extrême affaiblissement» (24). Despite temporary lapses caused by physical handicaps, Montherlant remained convinced that man's grandeur depends on his independence from supernatural forces and his confrontation with bitter realities. The author's consistent admiration for the heroes of antiquity, the Roman soldier-philosophers, is revealed theatrically in *La Guerre Civile.* In Act II, scene 4, Domitius tells Caton that the horrible element in suicide is not the dying but the risk of failure. He has noted, since his unsuccessful attempt, that he no longer has friends. Caton replies that in failing, Domitius has debased the noblest act of which man is capable. «L'homme n'a pas de droit plus sacré que celui de se supprimer s'il lui plaît. Et puis, on peut avoir été n'importe quoi: se tuer purifie tout» (25). In his *Postface,* Montherlant discerned in Roman philosophy «le courage, la gravité, l'infamie et la tristesse» (26). The courageous decision to annihilate oneself when no further sensual or creative pleasure can occur is comparable to the suicide of a Roman philosopher-general facing defeat. Montherlant always toyed with the idea of destroying his own literary efforts, but fortunately he did not. A recurring Montherlantian image, used even in his early essay, «Barrès s'éloigne», forms the epigraph of *La Marée du soir.* These last notebooks are appropriately introduced by the image of children building sand-castles at the seashore, erecting them during a warm summer's

(24) In *Aux fontaines du désir,* pp. 215-216.
(25) (Paris: Gallimard, 1965), p. 94.
(26) *Ibíd.,* p. 193.

day and then, with equal verve, joy and excitement, watching the castles disappear with the evening tide. To build and to destroy —life, work, what do they matter later? All that counts is the pleasure of the doing.

INDEX

Se terminó de imprimir en
la Ciudad de Madrid en el
mes de Octubre de 1977

studia humanitatis

1. LOUIS MARCELLO LA FAVIA, *Benvenuto Rambaldi da Imola: Dantista.* XII-188 pp. US $9.25.
2. JOHN O'CONNOR, *Balzac's Soluble Fish.* XII-252 pp. $14.25.
3. CARLOS GARCÍA, *La desordenada codicia,* edición crítica de Giulio Massano. XII-220 pp. $11.50.
4. EVERETT W. HESSE, *Interpretando la Comedia.* XII-184 pp. $10.00.
5. LEWIS KAMM, *The Object in Zola's* ROUGON-MACQUART.
6. ANN BUGLIANI, *Women and the Feminine Principle in the Works of Paul Claudel.* XII-144 pp. $9.25.
7. CHARLOTTE FRANKEL GERRARD, *Montherlant and Suicide.* XVI-72 pp. $5.00.

FORTHCOMING PUBLICATIONS

8. *Laclos. Critical Approaches to* Les Liaisons dangereuses. Ed. Lloyd R. Free.
9. *El cancionero del Bachiller Jhoan Lopez,* edición crítica de Rosalind Gabin.
10. JEAN J. SMOOT, *A Comparison of Plays by John M. Synge and Federico García Lorca: The Poets and Time.*
11. LOPE DE VEGA, *El amor enamorado,* critical edition of John B. Wooldridge, Jr.
12. *Studies in Honor of Gerald E. Wade,* edited by Sylvia Bowman, Bruno M. Damiani, Janet W. Díaz, E. Michael Gerli, Everett Hesse, John E. Keller, Luis Leal and Russell Sebold.
13. HELMUT HATZFELD, *Essais sur la littérature flamboyante.*
14. MARIO ASTE, *La narrativa di Luigi Pirandello: Dalle novelle al romanzo «Uno, Nessuno, e Centomila».*
15. JOHN A. FREY, *The Aesthetics of the* ROUGON-MACQUART.